DESIRE

Why It Matters

Books by Traleg Kyabgon

Integral Buddhism: Developing All Aspects of One's Personhood, Shogam Publications, 2018

King Doha: Saraha's Advice to a King, Shogam Publications, 2018

Letter to a Friend: Nagarjuna's Classic Text, Shogam Publications, 2018

Song of Karmapa: The Aspiration of the Mahamudra of True Meaning by Lord Rangjung Dorje, Shogam Publications, 2018

Moonbeams of Mahamudra: The Classic Meditation Manual, Shogam Publications, 2015

Karma: What it is, What it isn't, and Why it matters, Shambhala Publications, 2015

Four Dharmas of Gampopa, KTD Publications, 2013

Asanga's Abhidharmasamuccaya, KTD Publications, 2013

Ninth Karmapa Wangchuk Dorje's Ocean Of Certainty, KTD Publications, 2011

Influence of Yogacara on Mahamudra, KTD Publications, 2010

The Practice of Lojong: Cultivating Compassion through Training the Mind, Shambhala Publications, 2007

Mind at Ease: Self-Liberation through Mahamudra Meditation, Shambhala Publications, 2004

Benevolent Mind: A Manual in Mind Training, Zhyisil Chokyi Ghatsal Publications, 2003

The Essence of Buddhism: An Introduction to Its Philosophy and Practice, Shambhala Publications, 2002 & 2014

DESIRE
Why It Matters

Traleg Kyabgon

Foreword by Ringu Tulku Rinpoche

SHOGAM
PUBLICATIONS
2019

Shogam Publications Pty Ltd
PO Box 239 Ballarat, Victoria, Australia, 3353
www.shogam.org
info@shogam.com

Copyright © 2019 Felicity Lodro
First Edition

Printed in Australia and the United States of America

Edited by Traleg Khandro
Designed by David Bennett

National Library of Australia
Kyabgon, Traleg, 1955
Desire: Why It Matters

Printed book ISBN: 978-0-6481293-1-8 (Paperback)
E-book ISBN: 978-0-6481293-2-5

DEDICATION

To the remarkable succession of Traleg Tulkus
who have graced and continue to grace the
world with their wisdom and compassion.

Contents

PART TWO: ABHIDHARMA—THE PSYCHOLOGY OF
MEDITATION

Foreword

I am most grateful to Traleg Khandro and the team at Shogam Publications for bringing out the precious teachings of Traleg Kyabgon Rinpoche in this book *Desire: Why It Matters*. I have no doubt that Rinpoche's insightful and clear explanation of some often misunderstood aspects in Buddhism would benefit many readers.

In this book *Desire: Why It Matters*, Traleg Kyabgon Rinpoche discusses the notion of desire from Buddhist and other perspectives. He reviews commonly held beliefs of desire that are often misguided and can be diametrically opposed. On the one hand there is the belief that desire is an important human experience that is natural, which leads to happiness and pleasure. Then there is the juxtaposition that desire is a type of demon whose expression leads to diminishment and destruction. There has been a long-standing belief in some Eastern and Western religious and philosophical traditions that all forms of desire are bad and that our ultimate goal is a state of complete desirelessness.

"The assumption of these traditions being, if we do not desire anything, we will not have any concerns. If we do not have any concerns, we will be completely content, and completely happy. That is not the view of Buddhism as I understand it, particularly in relation to the distinction between the ultimate goal of attaining enlightenment and the relative and more immediate aim of wanting to improve and elevate oneself.

There is a litany of human foibles, misdemeanors, and misconduct that comes from unmediated desire. When the desire is not controlled or managed effectively, it can manifest as a very destructive eruption. Nevertheless, we should not then conclude that we have to extinguish desire altogether. To overcome destructive or demeaning desires requires one to harness a stronger desire to motivate oneself towards a more positive direction and goal. This requires insight and skill to overcome highly habitualized tendencies that can lead to a type of entrapment, to then produce a positively motivated approach that allows one to desire freely producing enriched meaning, outcomes, and experiences." Author, Traleg Kyabgon Rinpoche.

Traleg Kyabgon explores the Buddhist notion of desire within its positive and negative forms, seeking to explode some myths and clarify some misunderstandings. The book is also designed to inspire the passion of the readers to seek a fulfilling life without needing to demean one's experience of desire.

I am confident that this book will become a life-changing guide to its readers.

Ringu Tulku Rinpoche
Founder,
Bodhicharya Centres and Organisations,
5th June 2019

Biography of Author
TRALEG KYABGON RINPOCHE IX

Traleg Kyabgon Rinpoche IX (1955-2012) was born in Nangchen in Kham, eastern Tibet. He was recognized by His Holiness XVI Gyalwang Karmapa as the ninth Traleg tulku and enthroned at the age of two as the supreme abbot of Thrangu Monastery. Rinpoche was taken to Rumtek Monastery in Sikkim at the age of four where he was educated with other young tulkus in exile by His Holiness Karmapa for the next five years.

Rinpoche began his studies under the auspices of His Eminence Kyabje Thuksey Rinpoche at Sangngak Choling in Darjeeling. He also studied with a number of other eminent Tibetan teachers during that time and mastered the many Tibetan teachings with the Kagyu and Nyingma traditions in particular, including the *Havajra Tantra*, *Guhyasamaja Tantra*, and the third Karmapa's *Zabmo Nangdon* (*The Profound Inner Meaning*) under Khenpo Noryang (abbot of Sangngak Choling). Rinpoche studied the *Abhidharmakosha*, *Pramanavarttika*, *Bodhisattvacharyavatara*, *Abhidharmasamuccaya*, *Six Treaties of Nagarjuna*, the *Madhyanta-vibhaga*, and the *Mahayanuttaratantra* with Khenpo Sogyal. He also studied with Khenpo Sodar and was trained in tantric ritual practices by Lama Ganga, who had been specifically sent by His Holiness Karmapa for that purpose.

In 1967 Rinpoche moved to the Institute of Higher Tibetan Studies in Sarnath, and studied extensively for the next five years. He studied Buddhist history, Sanskrit, and Hindi, as well as Longchenpa's *Finding Comfort and Ease* (*Ngalso Korsum*), *Seven Treasuries* (*Longchen Dzod Dun*), *Three Cycles of Liberation* (*Rangdrol Korsum*), and *Longchen Nyingthig* with Khenchen Palden Sherab Rinpoche and Khenpo Tsondru.

When Rinpoche had completed these studies at the age of

sixteen, he was sent by His Holiness Karmapa to study under the auspices of the Venerable Khenpo Yesha Chodar at Sanskrit University in Varanasi for three years. Rinpoche was also tutored by khenpos and geshes from all four traditions of Tibetan Buddhism during this time.

Rinpoche was subsequently put in charge of Zangdog Palri Monastery (the glorious copper colored mountain) in Eastern Bhutan and placed under the private tutelage of Dregung Khenpo Ngedon by His Holiness Karmapa to continue his studies of Sutra and Tantra. He ran this monastery for the next three years and began learning English during this time.

From 1977 to 1980, Rinpoche returned to Rumtek in Sikkim to fill the honored position of His Holiness' translator, where he dealt with many English-speaking Western visitors.

Rinpoche moved to Melbourne, Australia in 1980 and commenced studies in comparative religion and philosophy at LaTrobe University. Rinpoche established E-Vam Institute in Melbourne in 1982 and went on to establish further Centers in Australia, America, and New Zealand. For the next 25 years Rinpoche gave weekly teachings, intensive weekend courses, and retreats on classic Kagyu and Nyingma texts. During this time Rinpoche also taught internationally travelling extensively through America, Europe, and South East Asia and was appointed the Spiritual Director of Kamalashila Institute in Germany for five years in the 1980's.

Rinpoche established a retreat center, Maitripa Centre in Healesville, Australia in 1997 where he conducted two public retreats a year. Rinpoche founded E-Vam Buddhist Institute in the U.S in 2000, and Nyima Tashi Buddhist Centre in New Zealand 2004. In 2010 Rinpoche established a Buddhist college called Shogam Vidhalaya at E-Vam Institute in Australia and instructed students on a weekly basis.

Throughout his life Rinpoche gave extensive teachings on many aspects of Buddhist psychology and philosophy, as well as comparative religion, and Buddhist and Western thought. He was an active writer and has many titles to his name. Titles include: the best selling *Essence of Buddhism*; *Karma, What It Is, What It Isn't, and Why It Matters*; *The Practice of Lojong*; *Moonbeams of Mahamudra*; and many more. Many of Rinpoche's books are translated into a number of different languages including Chinese, French, German, Korean, and Spanish. Rinpoche's writings are thought provoking, challenging, profound, and highly relevant to today's world and its many challenges.

Rinpoche was active in publishing during the last two decades of his life, beginning with his quarterly magazine *Ordinary Mind*, which ran from 1997 to 2003. Further, Rinpoche founded his own publishing arm Shogam Publications in 2008 and released a number of books on Buddhist history, philosophy, and psychology and left instructions for the continuation of this vision. His vision for Shogam and list of titles can be found at www.shogam.com.

Rinpoche's ecumenical approach can be seen in his other activities aimed at bringing buddhadharma to the West. He established the biannual Buddhism and Psychotherapy Conference (1994 - 2003), and Tibet Here and Now Conference (2005), and the annual Buddhist Summer School (1984 to the present).

Traleg Kyabgon Rinpoche IX passed into parinirvana on 24 July 2012, on Chokhor Duchen, the auspicious day of the Buddha's first teaching. Rinpoche stayed in meditation (*thugdam*) for weeks after his passing. A traditional cremation ceremony was conducted at Maitripa Centre and a stupa was erected on the center's grounds in Rinpoche's honor.

It is a privilege to continue Rinpoche's vision and initiatives, and to continue to make the profound teachings of Traleg Kyabgon Rinpoche IX given in the West for over 30 years available through his Centers' activities and Shogam Publications. Rinpoche's Sangha hope that many will benefit.

Acknowledgements

I first and foremost wish to thank the brilliant and remarkable Traleg Kyabgon Rinpoche IX for leaving such a rich legacy of over 30 years of Dharma teachings given during his time in the west. Rinpoche's teachings continue to nurture and enrich so many lives in so many ways around the world and I will be forever grateful to Rinpoche for his unending and tireless work.

One of the measures of the quality of Rinpoche's work lies in its ability to transform the recipient, and I have personally been moved and changed through this editing process. I hope others will benefit from these beautiful teachings. I wish to thank the many transcribers who diligently recorded every word spoken by Rinpoche in order for this book to be produced. To Salvatore Celiento for his undying support, excellent eye for detail, and tremendous assistance with the technical and Sanskrit terms. Also to Lyn Hutchison for her assistance with the technical and Sanskrit terms. To Claire Blaxell for her insight, patience, and profound command of the English language. To the very talented David Bennett for his wonderful cover design and for formatting the book so beautifully. And to you the reader, I hope with all my heart that the enriching qualities of desire are part of your spiritual journey.

Traleg Khandro

Editor's Introduction

I want to make this introduction brief, mainly because I do not wish to delay the reader from delving into the wonderful teachings by Traleg Kyabgon Rinpoche presented herein. Often, it can be believed that striving and passion for life, wishing for greater things in life, and loving intensely can somehow be an obstacle on the path to enlightenment, almost as if the best way to speed up the enlightenment journey is to add in a good dose of self-flagellation. Further, it can also be thought that to avoid too many experiences or responsiveness to life can be cleansing and speed up the spiritual journey. In this book, Rinpoche challenges the idea that experiencing less intensity, being non-attached to everything, being desireless, and being emotionless would somehow enrich the spiritual journey. Rinpoche addresses some aspects of the Buddhist theory that he considers have been misapprehended by some outside of Buddhism and even some within it.

In Rinpoche's discussion on aspects of Abhidharma, the Psychology of Meditation, Rinpoche asks us to consider our psychological complexity, and he pieces apart for us many of the elements that collectively create experience and what we think of as "the mind." He asks us to be discerning and develop an understanding of the subtlety of the different manifestations of desire, emotion, and experience, both those that are inculcated with diminishing qualities, and those that are positive and uplifting. He asks us to get to know ourselves better and to understand that on the path to enlightenment, we do not need to get rid of anything as such, but rather, we need to empower ourselves through enhancing our positive desires and emotions, which automatically in turn diminishes the strength and hold some negative habitual tendencies can have over us. He asks us not to try and walk a colorless path to enlightenment afraid that intensity of experience will somehow drop us into a lower state.

Enlightenment, Rinpoche reminds us, is expansive, vivid, and unbounded. He asks us to walk in the world brightly, not dimly. He asks us not to be afraid to fill our skin and embrace the opportunities we have for growth and positive experiences. Rinpoche reminds us of the immediate Buddhist goal of increasing happiness and reducing suffering as part of what our experience on the path should be. Rinpoche reminds us that enlightenment is a distant goal that requires work, but that in the meantime, and throughout such a journey, we should be enriched and our enjoyment of life should be magnified. Rinpoche states that Buddhism is all about relationships and in that and many other respects, we should not misunderstand what is meant by "non-attachment."

The journey of the meditator is a personal one that requires stark honesty about who we are at any given time, and that this honesty will serve us well to be able to quietly work on and transform weaknesses, discover new strengths, and develop a greater depth of character. This book contains aspects of Buddhist Psychology, the Abhidharma, that help piece apart how we apprehend the world. These traditional teachings were designed to ensure we develop an understanding of how human experiences are created and by so doing, it provides a clear approach to self-improvement. Demystifying the human experience through this understanding avails us the opportunity to fully embrace a real and untainted relationship with ourselves, others, and the world.

I have done my best to ensure that in editing this book I have not changed the meaning of Rinpoche's intended message. If I have, I ask for your forgiveness. Any errors are mine alone. I remain a humble and passionate student of the Dharma and I hope that you find, as I have in reading this book, a fresh approach to working on self-improvement and walking on the path for the benefit of others.

Traleg Khandro

DESIRE

Why It Matters

PART ONE

The Nature of Desire

Chapter 1
Ubiquitous Nature of Desire

In Buddhism, as individuals, we speak about attaining enlightenment as our ultimate goal. We can see this as our distant goal. Our more immediate or relative goal is to put our effort into improving ourselves as human beings, to increase happiness, and reduce suffering. So we have two sets of goals, as Buddhist practitioners. As human beings we may not particularly expect to become enlightened any time soon but the desire to attain enlightenment as our ultimate goal remains.

The demarcation line between the states of enlightenment and non-enlightenment is not as clear-cut as many may think. In Buddhism, enlightenment is not seen as a fixed state or place. That means that there are degrees of enlightenment. As a distant goal we wish to attain full enlightenment, the so-called, perfect state—that is, to attain Buddhahood.

Before we attain Buddhahood we can still work towards becoming more enlightened than less. That is, we can learn to elevate ourselves. In Tibetan it is called 'phags pa; in Sanskrit, ārya. Ārya means "to be elevated"; 'phags pa has the same connotation. As ordinary human beings, if we have not embarked on the spiritual or Dharmic path[1] to seek clarity and self-improvement, then our situation may not improve. Without effort, it is said, we can remain in confusion, led by our mental affliction.

Leaving Imprints in the Mind

In Buddhism, we say that our mental afflictions consist of what we call "emotional conflicts," such as excessive desire, anger, jealousy, envy, pride, excessive egocentricity, and other similar mental events. So when the mind is disturbed by these afflictions, according to Buddhism we become more and more confused and entrenched in our way of thinking, behaving, and experiencing things—that is, our experiences lose their freshness. Our openness of mind or flexibility in how we relate to ourselves and others then becomes compromised and eroded.

Whatever we experience leaves imprints in our mind. This in turn establishes strong patterns of behavior in how we use our thoughts, how we express positive and negative emotions, how we express our anger, unbridled desires, craving, grasping, and so forth. These habitualized behaviors lead to what, in Buddhism, is called "fixation[2]."

Strongly habitualized patterns of behavior set up tendencies whereby we begin to behave in a very predictable fashion. These habits, once established, do not stay the same but tend to become more intensely fixed and inflexible. It is not as if a certain level of negative and unwholesome habits becomes established and we just continue to operate at that level. Instead, as time progresses, the habits can gradually get more deeply ingrained and worsen. This can result in a person becoming more prone to agitation or allowing oneself to be more troubled by negative forms of emotion, whether it be jealousy, anger, or frustrations of any kind. The agitation is perpetuated in forms of unsatisfied desire. To allow oneself to remain in that state is described in the teachings as "a state of degradation." As previously mentioned, the concept of ārya means we need to learn to rise. To "raise" oneself means to break out of these negative habit-patterns, these well-entrenched ways of thinking and behaving. To do that, we need to learn to reduce and eventually go beyond grasping and fixation[3]. It is the grasping and fixation that contribute to habits becoming more and more entrenched. It is because of grasping and fixation that we return repeatedly to the same way of seeing and responding to things. As it is said in the teachings, due to our confusion we think that if we can satisfy the desires that we have, they will remain satisfied and we will gain peace of mind.

For example, if one desires more money, satisfying that desire does not make the desire for money go away. In fact, that desire will often increase. So it is with many other forms of desire. Another example is food: by eating more, the appetite for food does not diminish. The more one eats the more one tends to throw oneself into food. One's appetite increases. The habit of wanting to devour food becomes stronger. It is the same with other negative patterns of behavior.

Therefore, from the Buddhist point of view, we need to understand the significance of grasping and fixation and its influence on our state of well-being, in order to overcome it. Grasping comes from not knowing how to handle our emotional responses and experiences. Fixation, on the other hand, has a conceptual or intellectual component that comes from holding onto certain kinds of beliefs within a conceptual framework. Thus, grasping and fixation are seen as being connected to the management of excessive or unbridled desire.

Desire that Uplifts and Desire that Degrades

There is a tendency by many to think that Buddhism is about extinguishing desire—that is, not to have any kind of desire at all. The ultimate state of liberation is often described as the attainment of a desireless state. Therefore, many people see some kind of paradox in what Buddhists are trying to attain. If Buddhists desire a state of desirelessness, then it is a paradox. How can one desire the state of desirelessness? As long as you desire the state of desirelessness, there is going to be desire. In fact, we can look at and understand desire differently. In Buddhism we make the distinction between different types of desire. Not all desires are the same, nor do we need to extinguish all desires. What Buddhism instructs is to distinguish certain forms of desire from other forms of desire; those that degrade us and those that uplift us. Some forms of desire are extremely helpful and can assist in our transformation.

From the Buddhist point of view, if we can distinguish between different types of desire, then we can see what forms of desire lead to craving, grasping, fixation, and clinging, and what types of desire do not lead to craving, grasping, fixation, and clinging.

Fundamentally, positive desires do not re-impose our negative habit-patterns. Certain forms of desire are far more likely to lead to the experience of contentment, satisfaction, and fulfillment.

If we had no desire at all, there would be no motivation, there would be no will to do anything. Apathy would take over. Everything would become ordinary, insignificant, or meaningless. Through developing understanding of these distinctions, we can learn to utilize desire to overcome its more negative forms.

For the individual to be motivated on the spiritual path, we have to make use of the concept of progression. We need to progress on the path. We cannot just simply stay content with wherever we are. It is not about saying "I'm just going to learn to accept who I am and where I am and leave it at that." We have to have aspirations, we have to set goals. The concept of striving is an important concept within Buddhism—striving towards attaining certain goals, improving oneself, going forward, being motivated, feeling vigorous and energized. All of these things are positive motivating forces that require desire.

From the Buddhist point of view, we need to learn to utilize desire in such a positive way that we can overcome the negative, destructive aspects of desire through positive motivation and activity. The destructive elements come from excessive desires in all their forms—excessive desires such as greed. Even from an ordinary everyday point of view, we understand the dangers associated with uncontrolled, excessive, and unbridled desires.

There is a litany of human foibles, misdemeanors, and misconduct that is generated through uncontrolled desire. When the desire is not controlled, not managed, it can manifest as very destructive. But on that account we should not then conclude that we have to overcome desire altogether.

The Theory of Desirelessness

There are traditions in both the east and the west that say that all forms of desire are bad and that we need to overcome desire and attain a state of complete desirelessness. "If we don't desire anything, we will not have any worries. If we do not have any worries, we will be completely content, completely happy." From a Buddhist point of view as stated in the very beginning of this book, we first need to make the distinction between the ultimate goal of attaining enlightenment and the relative, more immediate goal of wanting to elevate oneself, remembering that enlightenment is a distant goal.

In Buddhism, what becomes clear is that while enlightenment may be a desireless state and this will be discussed in more detail later in the book, we cannot afford to extinguish all forms of desire, within our endeavor of self-elevation or self-improvement. Therefore, when we speak about grasping, clinging, and fixation, we are referring to negative forms of desire that lead to negative experiences. The desire to cultivate and uplift ourselves through generating positive fulfilling emotions and wholesome states of mind is considered to be very important.

So the question we need to ask is "how do we overcome negative habit-patterns?" In brief, we overcome negative habit-patterns by developing the motivation to act in such a way that goes counter to the established habits. Going against what we are used to doing habitually is, in a nutshell, how we overcome established habits. If we do not have a strong desire to do that, we will suffer from weakness of will. Desire and will, or determination, go together to overcome negative habits and to elevate our experiences. If we do not have any desire at all, we will not have the will to progress.

Strengthening Desire to Overcome Bad Habits

Even if there is some kind of interest, some kind of vague notion that "I must change my ways," or "I should really start to do something about not eating so much," or "I need to address my laziness"—the only way we are going to succeed in controlling our excessive appetites and entrenched behaviors is by exercising will. In other words, what one is trying to do is create a stronger desire for *not* reaching for food than the desire to reach for the food. Gradually one is learning how to harness positive desire so that one can develop the willpower necessary to overpower and overwhelm the negative desires that we have: negative appetites, excessive passions, negative states of mind and mental attitudes, negative way of perceiving things, negative view of oneself, negative views we harbor of other human beings and other aspects of our world, and of our own experience.

How can we overcome all of these negativities and excesses? As mentioned, we can do that by learning to harness the positive forms of desire in such a way that we develop the necessary willpower to deal with the entrenched habits that can be very difficult to overcome. The point is if we really harness positive kinds of desire, we can succeed in overcoming negative habit-patterns, and thus elevate ourselves and our experiences. If we learn to use desire in a positive manner, it will not lead to fixation. In Buddhism, the way one does this is to see everything from the point of view of the dynamic nature of our human emotions, the dynamic nature of our human experiences. When we get involved in negative thoughts, negative states of mind, we do not see the dynamism. We view everything in a very static and fixed way. If we practice utilizing our positive desires, we can see everything we are experiencing or going through in relation to its transformative potentiality. Whatever experience we have has the potential to be transformed.

That is to say, whatever emotion or thought we have contains the inherent capacity and opportunity for us to experience that same emotion or thought in a different way, in a transformed way. That possibility is enhanced when we are not doggedly stuck in negative forms of mind. When we are highly fixated, we can get completely immersed and caught up in negative forms of desire. This fixation can remove the opportunity for transformation at that time. We can then only expect more of the same—unchallenged negative habit-patterns that become more entrenched and gradually get worse over time. One can sink more deeply into states of agitation and into our basic mental disturbances. The more deeply entrenched a state we are in, the harder it can be to change. There can eventually be a diminished potential for transformation.

If we have the will and determination and a certain goal in mind when dealing with our negative states of mind, even when those negative states come up in our mind, even though the same negative states have arisen—we have the potential to produce something different from that experience. By relating to the same experience differently rather than having the same response all over again we can metamorphose the outcomes. That means that the potentiality for change can be developed from the same habitual responses, experiences, and patterns.

If we have the necessary willpower and develop an understanding of how to use our positive desires in the correct way, we do not transform only the positive states of mind. We do not then only have positive thoughts and emotions arising. Our old habitual thoughts and emotional patterns of behavior are likely to continue to arise. If they arise in an environment where we have clear goals in mind, then with the help of techniques, meditational practices, use of analysis, etcetera—the same thoughts, emotions, and feelings enter a different mental environment that allows for transformation.

What we are aiming for in Buddhism, rather than the extinguishment of all desires, is to learn to overcome the negative forms. We are looking at the purification of desires rather than the abandonment of all desire. The process of abandonment and that of purification are completely different. Buddhist practice, which involves overcoming clinging, grasping, and fixation, is designed to aid in the process of purifying our desires. It is not there to make us abandon desire altogether because, as previously stated, if there were no desire at all, we would have no will and determination so little if anything would be accomplished. We may attain the state of *apatheia* and that is not the goal!

An early British Buddhist scholar called Mrs. Rhys-Davids was very strong on this point, saying that Buddhism instructs that we should overcome *taṇhā*. Taṇhā means "thirst" which in this context is referring to craving. When we do not know how to differentiate positive kinds of desire from negative kinds it is said to be like drinking salt water in order to quench thirst—of course, we know that drinking salt water will increase thirst. In a similar way, if we do not know how to handle our desires properly, it will only make our hunger deeper and our thirst even more intense.

If we can learn to deal with our desires properly, we will find satisfaction and fulfillment. From this point of view, if we can learn to distinguish negative forms of desire, like taṇhā, from the positive ones and cultivate positive desires, we can learn to find satisfaction.

In that respect, desire is central to spiritual practice. We may desire certain things from our meditation practice and other forms of spiritual practice and these desires can be fulfilled. If we continue to indulge in negative forms of desire, those desires become more intense. Negative desires by their very nature cannot be satisfied. If we can practice and develop a type of non-grasping and non-fixation through our Buddhist practice, even while we continue to enjoy certain objects of desire, those desires can eventually cease to give rise to taṇhā or thirst. Managed desires can cease to give rise to habitualized and non-habitualized grasping and fixation.

As the Buddha said, it is not the objects of desire that trap us. It is not the beautiful object that we see. It is not the pleasurable sound that we hear, or the pleasant scent that keeps us entrapped. Rather, it is our response to these things. If we can learn to differentiate positive desires from negative ones and associate positive desires with willpower, to try to bring about a degree of transformation in our attitude, in how one experiences things, then gradually, that may not bring about the same reactions in us. In other words, over time, this grasping tendency would not arise or would not arise as intensely.

We should not think that grasping and fixation are overcome by just not engaging in any kind of willful activity or by simply disengaging. From a Buddhist perspective, by disengaging we will not attain quietude where all desires extinguish. That is not the Buddhist view, even though many people think of the Buddhist approach to desire in that way. In Buddhism we emphasize the notion of meditation and meditational peace of mind. Meditational peace of mind goes hand-in-hand with positive forms of desire. The negative desires destabilize our mind and the positive forms of desire help to stabilize our mind and bring about peace of mind, as a consequence of that.

Desiring Desirelessness

There is no paradox in desiring a desireless state. I am not necessarily saying that desirelessness cannot be attained. In Buddhism, we can use positive forms of desire in order to overcome negative forms of desire and that process is how we learn to transcend desire. We are not directly desiring a desireless state. We are not saying that by desiring a desireless state we will attain a state of desirelessness.

Using the example of food again, it is possible to desire *not* to desire something. It is possible to desire not to desire chocolate pudding, for example. If that desire for not desiring chocolate pudding gets stronger, the desire for chocolate pudding diminishes. There is no paradox in that either. We can desire not to desire something and we may succeed.

The main criterion for distinguishing whether a desire is uplifting and positive or degrading and negative is whether there is an intense craving, grasping quality to it or not. From a Buddhist point of view, when there is a lot of grasping, clinging, and fixation involved in our desires, that befuddles our mind somewhat. We start to fantasize and fabricate things. The basic criterion for whether we are getting too caught up in our experience whatever it might be, depends on how it is exaggerated in the mind and the degree of destabilizing it creates.

Defining the Terms, "Need," "Want," and "Desire"

Generally speaking: *need* has to do with the necessities of life. We need enough to eat, shelter, clothes to keep us warm, human relationships, social intercourse, and so on; *desire*, as discussed, is more amorphous as there are many forms of desire; *want* is a decision we make about what we wish to obtain. From a Buddhist point of view, both "desire" and "want" can be modified.

We can train ourselves to want what we really need and not want those things we do not need. Learning to distinguish the things that are good for us and learning not to want the things that are bad for us is the key. Related to the categories of what we find desirable and what we do not find desirable is learning not to want certain things even if they are desirable; and learning how to want something even if it is not desirable. Furthermore, it is important to keep in mind that things that are not desirable currently may become desirable later on with a change in approach and attitude. It is about having the same experience but managing it differently. Handling an experience or situation differently will bring a different result. That is, having the same experience but managing that experience in a different way can bring a different result.

From a Buddhist point of view, whatever negative habit we have to overcome by using our willpower, which comes from harnessing the more positive forms of desire, will allow us to transform. So we can still have that negative experience without feeling discouraged. In that way we are more empowered to deal with it. This approach diminishes the effects of certain habits on our well-being. The concept of the diminution of the effects of certain habits only makes sense if we have the same experience but are relating to it differently. By approaching a difficult habit with a positive outlook so as not to be discouraged helps defuse the intensity or heaviness of the experience and its effect is then lessened.

Overcoming a bad habit is not about not having that experience arise anymore. That is not generally how habits are overcome. Bad habits are overcome through constant erosion of that deep-seated habit-pattern so the hold it has on us becomes less and less. It is not about still having or not having certain habit-patterns. It is about changing the combination of a strong habit and weak will to building stronger willpower to assist in weakening the effect a bad habit has upon our well-being.

Overcoming the effect of a bad habit seems to occur in stages: first, we recognize the effect of a bad habit and its hold upon our well-being. We see the strong habit in combination with a weak will; then as we build our willpower the two can become somewhat equal. That is, the habit is strong and equally the willpower has gained strength; once the willpower is stronger than the habit, the hold the habit has on us weakens. In that way we can overcome the diminishing effects the habit has upon us.

It is rarely possible to develop a degree of willpower out of nowhere in a vacuum and in one stroke make certain well-entrenched habits instantly go away. From a Buddhist point of view, by working toward developing a non-grasping and non-clinging attitude, we can consequently develop more willpower. The tendency to grasp, cling, and become fixated generates a sense of being unfulfilled, like an unquenchable thirst and this need for more and more constantly weakens our will.

From a Buddhist point of view, we can review our experiences in order to build the will to change. For example, we can look at how unsuccessful we are in satisfying our desires by doing the same thing again and again. We can see our endeavors and recognize that they are doomed to failure right from the beginning. Inculcating that thought in us will give rise to our power of will. We just need to realize the approach does not bring about fulfillment—like recognizing that drinking salt water will not satisfy thirst.

There is a difference between how we overcome grasping and clinging and how we overcome fixation. First, we have to overcome clinging and grasping; clinging and grasping are overcome by developing willpower and harnessing the positive forms of desire.

Fixation is overcome by learning not to get too caught up with the antidote to the bad habit and generate more and more willpower, because that can develop another kind of obsession, a new fixation. Rather, when the habit is weakened by positive willpower, we then need to leave any notion of obsession behind. We need to let go of the idea of the habit having a hold on us or that we need to be totally free of experiencing an old habit, to overcome it. We can see the old habit in a more relaxed fashion without fixation. It can be difficult to deal with old habits without slipping into fixation, particularly if one has not dealt with the grasping and clinging aspect, because it is very easy to just slide back into old habits.

Sometimes we may succeed, sometimes we may not, but that is the whole point of overcoming the habit. Those times when we do succeed will help to loosen the habit-pattern's hold on us. When we do not succeed, we should not put ourselves down or be too negative. This type of response can develop into a new fixation and a tendency for self-criticism. The point is having the desire to stop and then harnessing that desire. The main concern is not that sometimes we fail, submit, and yield to our desire or the object of our desire.

It is not about not experiencing things we wish we did not desire. Even while we are experiencing such desire, we can observe that experience to see what is going on in the mind. Even if sometimes we cannot resist and give in, that is still part of the practice. We should not see that as a failure, particularly.

If we are able to retain an ability to observe our responses and mental activity that relate to the desire, we can see that as part of the overcoming process. That observation and mindfulness is part of the practice because we need to experience when we fail and when we succeed, to help build an understanding of the distinction between the two experiences. This will enhance our understanding of the mind and how desire manifests. Those times when we cannot resist, we recognize that but we do not need to put ourselves down and feel bad. We just go back to desiring to be enriched rather than diminished and then the desire to stop becomes stronger than the habit itself.

Meditation, Thoughts, and Willpower

It is important in meditation not to equate thoughtlessness with meditation and thoughts with non-meditation. Whether you are in meditation or not in meditation should be judged by whether you are aware of your thoughts or not. If you become aware of the fact that many thoughts are coming up, that is part of meditation, even if it means that we are mindful and aware of unceasing and incessant thoughts.

If we approach meditation in this way, thoughts and activity in the mind will generally disturb us less. Sometimes our thoughts of wanting to get rid of thoughts intensify the disturbance in the mind during meditation. In that respect, we should try to put our effort into developing stronger mindfulness and not channel that energy into trying to stop thinking. If we channel our energy into establishing mindfulness and making that stronger, then our meditation will improve. That will be more effective than trying too hard not to think while meditating. Sometimes we end up obsessively thinking about not thinking and so then we just end up going around in a circle.

So we use our willpower to develop mindfulness. If we have mindfulness, that is meditation. From a Buddhist point of view, meditation is about mindfulness. It is not about going into a trance state. In all schools of Buddhism the real meditation is about mindfulness. Even though you can attain trance states through the practice of meditation—and in Buddhism that is also acknowledged and recognized—that is not the goal of meditation. In Buddhism the goal of meditation is to stabilize the mind. If we can stabilize the mind, we are having a successful meditation. We stabilize the mind with the practice of mindfulness.

So we should not concern ourselves too much about such things as incessant thoughts. In that respect, using willpower to stop thinking in meditation is not particularly helpful. We will achieve better results by using our willpower to be *mindful* in meditation. In meditation, mindfulness is described as the ability to return to the object of meditation whenever we find ourselves distracted.

"Non-forgetfulness" is another term used for mindfulness. That is, when we realize we are distracted, we remember to return to the object of meditation, whether the object is the breath or an actual object.

Non-fixation is harder to practice than non-grasping and non-clinging because it is subtler. Fixation is a more subtle form of grasping. In Buddhism, fixation has an intellectual component; it is more discursive or cognitive in nature.

Chapter 2
Apprehending the World through our Senses

In Buddhism, for example, in relation to the teachings on what are called the Twelve Interdependent Links, clinging and grasping are developed from feelings; feelings come from sense contact; sense contact arises from consciousness[4]. Part 2 of this book is devoted to explaining some of these concepts such as sense consciousness in more detail. The idea is that if we understand how the mind works in more detail, we are in a much better position to reduce suffering. Our focus in part 1 is to understand how desire arises and how we can use desire to uplift us and propel us forward on the spiritual path.

Because we are sentient, we come in contact with sensory objects through our visual, audial, and nasal senses. From that contact arises feelings of pain and pleasure. We are judging the experience through our senses and we conclude that this is painful, or this is pleasurable. From what we find pleasurable arises craving, craving for more of the same. "I find this pleasurable, I want to see more of this, I want to hear more of this sound, I like this smell." From craving arises grasping. This is how it is described in the teachings on the Twelve Interdependent Links. Clinging and grasping arise from desire. Desire is developed due to our responsiveness to feelings of pain and pleasure, "I like this, I don't like this." That discriminatory capacity comes from consciousness, being sentient. One then makes a distinction between what is pleasurable and what is not. So that is how the arising of desire through the senses can be understood.

Grasping and clinging can develop into fixation in a different way from what normally might be expected. We have feelings based on conscious discrimination—something is pleasurable, something is not pleasurable—and from that arise the experiences of clinging, grasping, attraction, and aversion. What we find attractive, what we are attracted to we chase after and latch onto. We do this both externally or physically, and within the mind, through our responsiveness. What we find unpleasant we develop aversion towards and that easily becomes habituated. We will tend to recoil and want to escape from that. That does not suggest, however, that we then do not experience grasping and fixation. In Buddhism, desire and a tendency towards grasping and clinging is seen as more ubiquitous than we might normally imagine. We grasp and cling even onto things that we have aversion to. Desire, clinging, grasping, and fixation are in fact more ubiquitous than anger, resentment, hostility, and bitterness. When we become bitter, resentful, or experience other conflicting emotions, there is an element of grasping, clinging, and fixation within these more negative experiences as well.

With the idea of consciousness, contact, and the sensory responsiveness that gives rise to attraction and aversion, we find we want to grasp onto what we are attracted to and cling to it. That same tendency to grasp and cling manifests in response to most experiences, be they positive, negative, or neutral. That is why grasping, clinging, and fixation are considered so ubiquitous within the sentient experience. This includes things that we hate and dislike. So aversion is just as likely to develop obsession and fixation that refuels our response to hating or not liking something.

In terms of our sensory experiences, the very moment we encounter a certain sense object our response can bring an immediate feeling of revulsion. This response is as much physical as it is mental. In Buddhism, a practitioner needs to work with this tendency, this preponderance towards grasping and clinging, precisely because of its pervasiveness.

Grasping and clinging arises in so many different contexts and in so many different ways, not just in terms of attraction and aversion. It arises even in terms of what we think about, what we believe in, how we believe in the reality of things, how we conceptualize about our self and the world, and how we develop certain convictions and fixate on them. We can become totally attached to our cherished belief systems and notions of how things are.

The Meaning of Wrong View, Right View, and Transcending View

In Buddhism we speak about wrong view, right view, and the transcending of all views. These are discussed in Buddhism due to the pervasive tendency to grasp and cling onto and fixate on things. That is why so much emphasis is placed on grasping and clinging and on the importance of distinguishing positive forms of desire from negative forms.

With most experiences there is an element of desire. For example, if we hate something or hate somebody, there may be the desire to do harm. So the desire to do harm is a form of desire. There is grasping and clinging involved in that notion of wanting to harm somebody because that desire is sustained by a sense of obsession or fixation.

Negative forms of desire not only give rise to clinging and grasping, they also become intermingled with other forms of negative emotion and negative states of mind. That is why all the liberating experiences that Buddhism talks about are free of obsession. They are liberated due to the absence of grasping, clinging, and fixation.

Non-grasping, Non-clinging, and Non-attachment

It may seem that teachings on non-clinging, non-grasping, and non-fixation are suggesting that we should have no desire, thus equating non-grasping and non-clinging with a form of non-desire. However this is not the case. We can have desires that do not necessarily give rise to clinging or grasping. We can utilize our positive forms of desire in order to liberate ourselves from grasping and fixation. That is fundamentally why we need to overcome grasping and fixation.

From a Buddhist point of view, if we grasp too much, if we cling onto things too much in terms of our experiences, our negative emotions are encouraged to flourish. Therefore, we are thrown into an agitated state making us unable to maintain a sense of presence of mind or peace of mind.

We have all kinds of emotions because we have desire. Not all kinds of emotions that we experience are bad and not all experiences of emotions necessarily lead to disturbance of the mind. We need to overcome grasping tendencies because they lead to the development of negative forms of emotion. If we learn how to let go of this tendency and other extreme forms of attachment, however, we can have the experience of a whole gamut of emotions that will not lead to disturbances of the mind. In fact, they will lead to a more fulfilling, richer, and deeper experience of life.

When we are caught up in the different forms of negativity—negative states of mind and negative emotions driven by grasping and clinging—they fan the negative emotions which then become inflamed. The inflammation of the negative states of mind and negative emotions leads to disturbances.

If we do not grasp onto what we experience, we will still have emotions. We can have the experience of emotions without it leading to disturbances. It is often not thought of in this way. We may equate non-clinging, non-grasping, and non-attachment to a form of passivity, a way of retiring from the world, turning away from the world, and not being engaged, as if any form of engaging with the world can lead to disturbance. We can erroneously believe that engagement in the world automatically gives rise to certain forms of emotional response and that the emotional response will lead to disturbances of the mind. It is not seen in this way, from a Buddhist perspective.

In Buddhism it is considered that we can learn to engage with the world more fully with a non-grasping attitude. What is meant by "non-grasping"? If we experience anger or jealousy or have a similar experience, we do not need to get caught up with that experience. We do not need to become completely immersed in and attached to it. We do not need to give importance to it as if whatever we experience reflects reality, rather than seeing that we have interpreted our experience. Believing that whatever I am experiencing is how things are denies the subjective apprehension of the experience. The more disturbed we become with an experience, the less able we are to experience things in an untainted way. In Buddhism, we refer to reality as related to our experiences, in terms of how things actually are.

In Buddhism, we see our disturbances coming from not being able to see the world just as it is. In Tibetan it is *gnas lugs*, "how things are." We do not experience how things are, because when we experience our negative emotions very intensely, we become convinced that everything we experience is true and real. From a Buddhist perspective, it is considered that the greater the intensity of the experience, the less truth there is because more and more fabrication is built into the experience.

We are creating our own personal story and narrative. All the characters in that story have some semblance of, some tenuous relationship to the real characters we may be blaming for all of our misery and all of the things that we are going through. The fictitious characters that we have created in our mind have taken on a whole life and reality unto themselves and we believe in these stories. It is the creation of our own personal reality, quite separate from "how things are," that is the basis of our disturbances.

Our disturbances arise from such creations because we do not have presence of mind. We are unable to interact fully with the world or with other people because we get more and more caught up in our internal stories and dramas, based on our fictitious ideas. We have ideas about the world, ourselves in terms of how we appear physically, how we appear to ourselves and to others, what others think of us, and what we think about ourselves. The list of stories we create can be endless. This develops as a complete personal reality in our heads. From a Buddhist point of view, these are the reasons to begin recognizing and letting go of clinging and grasping.

There are moral or ethical dimensions to what we are discussing as well. Psychologically and practically, this approach to life is seen as totally futile and harmful to ourselves and others. If we cling onto things, if we become greedy, lustful, always dissatisfied, and so on, we become morally corrupt, and psychologically and spiritually we become disturbed. We lose touch with ourselves, and our inner being. To some extent we lose touch with external reality and we live in a fabricated world, which in Buddhism is called "samsara." Samsara is a world governed by excessive desires and uncontrolled emotions such as anger, jealousy, pride, and ignorance based on our misapprehension of the world through our senses.

For these reasons, we are instructed on the importance of learning to reduce grasping and clinging to begin to live a better life. From that point of view, learning to overcome grasping and clinging is not the same as learning to become desireless. It is not about learning to develop distaste for life. It is not about turning away from the world or disengaging from the world. The samsaric experience of the world is the disengaged state. That is a world fabricated by the deluded mind. When the mind is deluded, we cannot see things clearly.

Not seeing things clearly means we interpret what we see and experience in relation to what we believe. If we learn to grasp less and cling less, we can become more engaged with the world. We can see the world in a different way and experience the world more directly. We will still have experience, but our life experience will not lead to frustration, dissatisfaction, meaninglessness, emptiness, and confusion. It will lead to more fulfilling experiences that more closely reflect how things truly are. This can allow us to be more directly engaged with others as well.

Therefore, by developing non-grasping, and non-clinging attitudes, we are aiming toward two forms of transformation: one to do with transformation on the affective level, in terms of our emotional responses; and the other to do with conceptual or intellectual transformation.

So there are two different kinds of transformation in Buddhism. These correspond to what are referred to as the *two veils*: one is the veil of emotional conflict, *kleśāvaraṇa*; kleśāvaraṇa means "veil of conflicting emotions," *nyon mongs kyi sgrib pa* in Tibetan; the other is called *shes bya'i sgrib pa* or *jñeyāvaraṇa*, which means "conceptual veil" or "veil of conceptual confusion."

These two veils prevent us from seeing how things are in the world. Contrary to what many people believe, Buddhism is not about turning away from the world. There would be no point in emphasizing "seeing how things are in relation to the world" if Buddhists were seeking to be separate from the world. If that were the case, it would not matter how things were in the world because it would not be important. Rather, it is said that by learning to remove the veils of conflicting emotions and conceptual confusion, we will see how things are and, from that, whatever we experience will lead to our flourishing. We will develop as individuals.

If we continually allow ourselves to be influenced by the two veils, we cannot see the world as it is. Therefore, we are not really in the world in the authentic sense. In some ways we could say that we are not worldly enough. So what Buddhism is saying is that when we are governed by samsara, we are not worldly enough.

If we really want to be a worldly person, we need to learn to engage with the world more directly, to live less in our heads and be more open to the world so that we are genuinely interacting directly. Our samsaric tendency is to interact with the world via our self-generated stories about how the world is. It is more in relation to the semblance of the world that we have created. Due to the two veils—that of emotional conflict caused by primary delusions such as excessive desire, anger, jealousy, pride, and ignorance; and the veil of conceptual confusion brought on by the dualistic notion of ourself and others existing separately, according to our interpretation—we develop fixation, which comes from how we experience and apprehend the world through our perceptions, opinions, and prejudices. We become fixated on how we see ourselves, others, and the world, in relation to predetermined self-opinions.

Buddhism is not saying we should not have desire. It *does* mean that we should be alert to the danger of unchecked desire, as it can become excessive. If we do not put some kind of restraint on our excesses, all our experiences will lack fulfillment and lead to frustration and disappointment. One of the dangers of excessive desire, as previously stated, is desire's ubiquitous nature. Without some sense of contentment, fulfillment, and meaning, we may conclude our lives are not worth living, or become totally cynical or nihilistic. There can be great pain if everything we want or gain in life leads to dissatisfaction. In fact, there may not only be the desire for things in life but one may not even desire life at all and wish to put an end to everything that produces dissatisfaction through constant clinging and grasping.

The Impermanent Nature of Desire

As Buddhist practitioners, if we have not developed an understanding of desire and of how to handle positive and negative desires, it can lead to a sense of failure. So we need to recognize the association between the related topics of desire and death, and desire and impermanence, to assist us to overcome grasping and clinging. Everything that we desire in relation to objects of desire is impermanent, or transient. Everything that we desire cannot be possessed in a static form. Even when we manage to fulfill our desire, due to change, it cannot be possessed in the same way that we acquired it.

As an example, if we desire a chest of drawers we see in a furniture shop, even if we do not have the money for it, we purchase it on credit. After a few years, it is not going to look the same. The wear and tear may begin to frustrate the level of our satisfaction. We may begin looking for a new chest of drawers. We may never find the perfect chest of drawers. Such an example can be used for so many things in life.

Due to our lack of understanding of non-grasping and non-clinging, whatever we desire, even when we acquire it, will lead to dissatisfaction. If we recognize non-grasping and non-clinging, even if these tendencies persist, and they most likely will, we will cling less, we will grasp less, and we will be able to enjoy what we have more.

With less clinging and grasping, we can develop real appreciation as we recognize the transience of all things. Then, whatever is available one is able to appreciate. In Japanese culture they have great appreciation for the chrysanthemum as it only blooms for a short time. Because of that it is considered very beautiful.

If we learn to utilize our desire properly, whatever we desire, we can enjoy and delight in it fully while it is there. When it is there, we can be more fully engaged with it. If we are driven by clinging and grasping, we are more likely to desire what we do not have, and forget to enjoy what we have. Thus, as soon as we obtain something the enjoyment is diminished—that is, being always one step ahead but never in the present.

How to be in the present is about engaging with the world so that we are not excessively engaged in our fantasies, wishes, unfulfilled desires, and frustrations. Rather, we can be taking a moment to be with whatever it is that we really like, cherish, love, and enjoy without grasping too much. We need to develop the luxury of time to fully appreciate what is going on presently.

Enjoyment and grasping do not mix. We think grasping and clinging are what brings enjoyment. Clinging and grasping interferes with what we enjoy. We often do not have the time to enjoy what we consume even in terms of food. We can often be in a state of frenzy.

Non-grasping, non-clinging, and non-fixation are connected to appreciation, openness, joy, and all the positive qualities associated with life. Non-grasping, non-clinging, and non-fixation, instead of leading to lack of appreciation of life, leads to appreciation of life. For example, Buddhist monastics are instructed through their training to recognize the thirst and hunger that grasping, clinging, and excessive attachment brings. Throughout their training they work towards reducing this tendency and then with diligence they can come out the other end as a better person.

In summary, reducing or overcoming grasping, clinging, and fixation leads to greater appreciation of the world and of other human beings. When we are too clingy and "graspy," we can become more and more withdrawn and self-engrossed, as we become caught up in our own internal drama of pain and suffering. That is why, according to Buddhism, we do not need other people to cause us suffering. We manufacture plenty of home-grown suffering ourselves. Negative states of mind have a way of germinating and multiplying. Our negativities, self-pity, and despair have a way of generating more despair, more self-pity, and more comprehensive negative attitudes towards others and the world. Without anybody doing anything to us, we can become more and more caught up within ourselves.

That is why we learn not to grasp or cling too much through the practice of meditation, using mindfulness and awareness. Being mindful of how our mind works to create obsessions, we can release the hold these obsessions have on us and can then learn to appreciate others more and the world more. When we appreciate others and the world more, our life becomes enriched. When we are self-absorbed, we invariably return to something that is negative, either about oneself or about others. When we are engaged with the world more, we dwell less on negativities and then we can progress more easily.

To reiterate, Buddhist meditation should not be seen as a way of withdrawing from the world. Rather, it is a way of allowing us to break out of our own internal world. We learn to step out of that and engage with the world in a direct and an enriched way so that *śila*, ethical conduct, can manifest within a more meditative, less grasping frame of mind. It is important to think of training ourselves to grasp and cling less. This is the best way to manage our desire and behave more ethically.

From a Buddhist point of view, there is nothing wrong with the world, *per se*. What is wrong about our worldly experiences is the conflicting emotions that we experience and the conceptual confusion that we suffer from. These two aspects of our samsaric mind lead to clinging, grasping, and fixation. If we learn to have less grasping and so forth, everything that we experience about the world will be better.

From the Buddhist point of view, what is internal and what is external go together. They are not seen as entirely separate. From the Mahayana[5] point of view then, if we suffer a lot of frustration due to grasping and fixating, we are not in a good position to benefit or help others. Generally speaking, irrespective of any particular school or tradition of Buddhism, if we look at it properly, Buddhism does not disparage desire, *per se*. What Buddhism really emphasizes is the separation of negative forms of desire from positive forms of desire. It also emphasizes how to utilize the positive forms of desire in order to advance oneself on the spiritual path and also in relation to how to live one's life properly and interact with other human beings in a much more constructive and beneficial way.

If one had no desire, there would be no need for interaction, there would be no need for the world. That is not the goal of Buddhism. When we talk about overcoming desire, we are talking about negative forms of desire that are tied up with clinging, grasping, and fixation. If we do not become entangled with grasping, clinging, and fixation, we can act more freely. If we can act more freely, we can have desires. Those desires then will not lead to degradation of our lives but can add richness to our lives and make our lives more meaningful.

Utilizing positive desires to create positive willpower develops strength to overcome whatever it is that we need to overcome. Whether it is about practicing meditation more regularly, or wanting to develop certain qualities in oneself. Transformation comes from that combination of positive desire and positive willpower.

In other words, we do not need to focus our mind on what we believe we need to overcome. Rather, we should be focusing more on the desire for transformation than what we need to overcome. If we really make that desire very strong, it will generate its own power. It will develop the willpower we need for change and transformation.

When you have strong desires, it is important for them to be carefully managed. When we really want something, it has its own power. It has the power to destroy us, and also to uplift and enrich us. When that power is used positively, we can be transformed in a way that is of benefit to ourselves and others. When we desire the wrong thing very intensely, that can destroy us, and in that way we cannot contribute positively in the world and work to benefit others.

How strong is our will to change? If the will to change is really strong, one will change. If, however, you are thinking about all the things that you want to change, you may be discouraged and the will to change may become weak. You may think, "This is too much. I have a big problem on hand. How can I overcome this? I don't see any way out." Instead, if you focus more on the will to change than what you believe needs to change, it is less overwhelming and more power-inducing. Then you are positioning yourself for positive change.

For example, people who have been in car accidents can be told by doctors that they will never walk again. Some people start walking, not because they are thinking, "Oh, now I will never walk again; what a terrible thing! I can never overcome this physical limitation." It is more likely that they are thinking, "I *will* walk. I'm going to walk. I'll make myself walk," and then with that willpower they may be able to walk again. The same thing can happen in terms of our spiritual practice or in relation to our self-development.

If our will to change is strong enough, we will change. But if we are thinking about all the odds that we have to overcome, all the odds pitted against us, we may be discouraged and may not develop the will needed to transform ourselves. In Buddhism it is important that we work to recognize and be clear about our shortcomings. It is important to be clear about what we need to overcome. Having secured that self-knowledge there is then no benefit in dwelling on our shortcomings as that can diminish us. What we should be spending more time on is how to overcome our shortcomings to become a better person and have a better life experience, and further, to be in a position to benefit others.

Chapter 3
How Reality Challenges our Subjective Experience

Not becoming fixated on certainty is important. That does not mean that everything happens randomly. Rather, there is a pattern of change that we witness daily. Nevertheless, not demanding certainty from something that cannot deliver is the first step towards reducing grasping and fixation because that is how the world is. We can do our best to protect ourselves from change, but still, that will not change how the world is.

Even though the world is orderly in some ways, it is disorderly in other ways. There is interplay between orderliness and disorderliness when it comes to how the world works. We can develop openness to that interplay. Whenever a disruption occurs, we will be in a better position to handle it. We can develop more capability to manage difficulty which will help to avoid being completely devastated by hardship. In Buddhism, we believe that anything can happen. If we are open to that possibility, we will have greater capacity to deal with difficulty as we will not be in conflict with our fixed ideas of how the world should operate, compared to how it is actually manifesting. We will know better how to face circumstances as they present themselves.

If we can have more confidence in ourselves, even though we cannot predict what the world is going to do next, we are not thrown off-balance. But if we do not have balance within ourselves, even if the world behaves in an orderly fashion, we can still be thrown off-balance.

From the Buddhist point of view, we are not gods, we are not omnipotent so we cannot dictate how the world behaves. As individuals, if we cultivate ourselves and develop more wisdom about how the world works, adopt a higher and more compassionate view, we will see things differently and be able to develop more confidence. Then when disruptive things happen, we will not be thrown.

We can be more certain about ourselves than we can about the world if we cultivate such wisdom about how the world works. We can rely on our understanding in times of need and whenever we are in distress. Whenever things are not working out, we can tap into our inner resources. In other words, we will not be thrown into a sense of overwhelming loss—overwhelming feelings of loneliness, despair, rejection, and so on. It is not about not experiencing loss, but rather it is referencing not being completely overwhelmed by loss. Losing faith in ourselves, others, or the world is the least likely outcome when we have a better understanding of the unpredictable nature of the world of existence.

That is why we emphasize self-cultivation in Buddhism so that we can engage better with the world. Self-cultivation is perfected through the forgetfulness of the self as well, which is another interesting twist. We do not cultivate ourselves by being obsessed about the self. We do the opposite, and by cultivating ourselves without self-obsession, we can develop.

Then we develop and become richer as a person. But if we are self-absorbed in an egoistic fashion, we can become more negative and critical about ourselves and we become critical of other people also. Self-hatred is the natural outcome of getting too obsessed with oneself. We do not like ourselves—how we look, our attitudes, or our habits. From this state we can develop a dislike for other people and the world as well. We can develop a belief that everything has gone to the dogs, so to speak, and from that a nihilistic and cynical attitude can develop.

It can be important to take time for retreat or to cultivate ourselves in some way through study, contemplation, and meditation and in so doing avoid becoming self-absorbed. This can be enriching and provide an opportunity to develop insight into the human condition and the nature of reality. However, from the perspective of Mahayana Buddhism, we need to engage with others to develop ourselves fully. We cannot develop by ourselves, physically and mentally. Mentally and spiritually we need to think about others.

How we are treated by others is unpredictable. Sometimes they will treat us nicely, and other times they will not. We often do not know why we are being treated badly or, conversely, why we are being shown such kindness.

The point is that from our own side, if we are thinking about relating to others in a positive way, then we become richer as a person, and that is the key. The reward of relating well with others is found in how we grow within our understanding of and generosity towards others, and how we grow and develop ourselves. Such enrichment is not found in what they are doing for us or to us. Of course, being treated positively has a tremendous benefit. Whether the person responds in a positive way or not is secondary to the benefit we gain from approaching things in a positive manner without self-absorption.

This is true in relation to our family, friends, and in all types of situations. We are enriched if we are interacting in a positive and insightful way. In Buddhism, it is believed our actions and activities shape the kind of person we become. If we are doing things that are significant and meaningful, our life becomes enriched purely through that activity. The main point here is that whether our deeds are appreciated by the other person or not is of secondary concern.

By not conceptualizing and fixating on things too much, we learn to enjoy life more. *Discriminating awareness* is a term often used in Buddhism emphasizing the importance of discrimination on the path. We are human beings and we have to distinguish what is beneficial from that which is not beneficial. This of course includes distinguishing desirable forms of desire from non-desirable forms of desire, as previously discussed. We need to learn to discriminate in such a way that we avoid getting attached to or fixated on that discrimination as well. We can be discerning and still remain open and relaxed.

Normally, when we use our discriminating mind, our discriminations may not even correspond to the relative reality but rather may relate more to our predetermined beliefs, thoughts, and ideas. What is going on in our mind may not even correspond to what is occurring externally. Putting too many labels on what we experience creates a gap between our experience and whatever it is that we are experiencing. Too much conceptualization and too much judgment ruin our experience, as if nothing is good enough or not quite what we want. For example, you go to the beach and instead of just taking in the scenery and enjoying yourself, one ends up focusing on the terrible weather or on others making too much noise and so forth. So, the experience can be ruined through our ordinary discriminations and fixations.

In contrast, however, developing discriminating awareness allows us to experience things more fully by making choices about what is life-enhancing and what is not life-enhancing. For example, if we realize it is not good to conceptualize too much, we can reduce that activity and then relax and enjoy our experience more. That type of discrimination is very helpful. Conversely, if we are constantly judging, "this is good; that is bad; I want this; I don't want that" and so forth, we will remain dissatisfied.

If we are not engaged in what we are experiencing, we are also not engaged with the world. We can become caught up in our mind due to our excessive desire and excessive clinging and grasping. We have notions about how we like things: what a coffee should be like, what it means to have a holiday, what services a hotel should provide, and so forth.

A more relaxed, less fixated view of how things should be gives us a richer experience of life generally. That approach is also a form of discrimination. In Buddhism, it is not about making a choice between discrimination and non-discrimination. It is a choice between discrimination with attachment, grasping, and clinging, or discrimination without attachment, grasping, and clinging, or at least with less attachment, grasping, and clinging. Then our mind becomes less disturbed and perturbed.

The negativities that we experience, such as anger, have a way of growing if not managed well. An angry person becomes more and more angry, more and more resentful, more and more bitter as the years go by. An angry person can have more problems getting along with other people. Even forgetting spiritual possibilities—as Shantideva[6] and other male and female masters have said, even from a practical point of view, our life becomes diminished. The quality of life becomes diminished when we are too angry, too resentful, too unforgiving, and so forth. Some people do not forgive certain people for what they did 15 or 20 years ago. They are not hurting anybody other than themselves. That is what Buddhism teaches.

The people who are responsible for one's hurt are not being hurt by your resentment. Your resentment is only hurting yourself. If you are in a relationship and somebody leaves you and you cannot forget it, you cannot forgive that person, that person may not hurt, you are hurt. Grasping onto that experience only has one victim and that is you. From a Buddhist point of view, we want to learn not to grasp and cling as we are only damaging ourselves.

Even from a practical and psychological point of view, whether we believe in karma or not, we would still benefit from being able to be less fixated, with less clinging and grasping. It is important and worthwhile to contemplate this. It is too mono-focused to think we should not do certain things solely because of karma. That type of approach to karma lends additional weight to the notion that whatever we are doing may not be beneficial. It is far better to avoid doing certain things because they can be fundamentally harmful, knowing that if we continue with such behavior without correcting ourselves, then the habitual tendency will persist, deepen, and become more harmful to our well-being. So karma is not the sole reason to avoid doing certain activities.

In Buddhism we look at karma in a different way, particularly in a different way in relation to the Hindu approach. Karma in Buddhism is seen as less mechanical than it is otherwise often presented. It is based on the notion of probability—that is, given all the circumstances and factors at work at the current time, it is more probable that in the future a particular consequence may result. Rather than saying a particular thing will definitely happen, it is said there is a probability that it may arise[7].

Karma is important and it is important to respect it. When it comes to desire and the dimension of human experiences, apart from the Buddhist doctrinal side of things, there is a practical component to that, which can generate positive and uplifting behavior. What Buddhism suggests we should do is, more often than not, what we would want to do even if we were not Buddhist. This appears to be true in many respects.

Chapter 4
A Wrong View and a Right View to Satisfying Desire

Even though we need to go beyond grasping and fixation, that does not necessarily mean that we have to go beyond desire. Let us discuss non-fixation in a different context. The Buddhist perspective of how to purify desire helps to develop a clearer idea about its constructive use as well as some understanding of its destructive force. We can develop an understanding of both and of how to go beyond grasping, clinging, and fixation and attachment.

Desire, if unmanaged and unattended, can lead to ruin and self-destruction. Equally, if we use desire in order to transform ourselves, then desire also has a role to play even in the context of spiritual practice. Spiritual practice is not about going beyond all forms of desire. It is not as if all forms of desire necessarily lead to a state of samsaric imprisonment. Nor does desire necessarily perpetuate various forms of delusional thought, leading to conflicting emotions.

Certain positive forms of desire can be used in positive ways. The will to change and transform ourselves comes from utilizing desire in a constructive manner. Re-channeling our desires helps with motivation and the will to transform ourselves. We would not have any kind of willpower if it were not for strong desire. Not only can we make use of desire in a constructive fashion, with strong desire it can be even more constructive. Negative forms of strong desire lead to our ruin, but strong positive desires can lead to self-transformation. We can harness our strength, determination, resolve, and courage, through generating strong psychophysical power that comes from developing strong desires.

We really need to develop the right perspective on both the redemptive qualities and the perils associated with desire. Desire's dual nature has both the potential to liberate and transform, as well as to imprison, ensnare, trap, seduce, and lead us astray. From a Buddhist perspective, desire is not black and white or clear-cut. It is not the case that all desires are bad or that desire is a thing we do not have to worry about. We need a deeper understanding of how to harness positive forms of desire to weaken and overcome negative forms of desire. It is important not to downplay the dangers associated with negative forms of desire, on the one hand, and it is important not to ignore the potential liberating powers of desire, on the other. Realizing desire has a dual nature is very important.

The positive desires can lead us beyond grasping and clinging. Strong positive desires generate strong feelings. The intensity of desire does not necessarily lead to clinging, grasping, and fixation. We can develop strong positive energy that comes from desire through conscious cultivation, through consciously cultivating positivity. Grasping and clinging, and all the troubles associated with habituated obsessions come from a state which is not fully conscious.

In Buddhism, we believe our samsaric mind normally operates in a semi-conscious state. It is often compared to being half-asleep. Therefore, when we have experiences, we experience them in a half-conscious way and that is a conducive environment for grasping and clinging to develop. The quality of grasping and clinging does not necessarily come from the intensity of the experience, but rather, it comes from not being conscious and so not fully understanding what is going on.

Conscious cultivation of these positive states of mind and the cultivation of positive forms of desire, even if the experiences are intense, will not lead to grasping and the preponderance for getting caught up with all kinds of mental fixation. We can overcome our tendency to grasp and cling onto things and experiences by cultivating positive desires alone. We need to do more than that. We also need to overcome fixation.

Overcoming the tendency to grasp and cling is derived from learning to overcome fixation. This comes from the cultivation of what is often called "right view" in Buddhism. Grasping, clinging, and fixation are connected to what we call "wrong view." The mindset of non-attachment, non-grasping, and non-clinging, unpolluted by the excessive experience of anger, resentment, bitterness, egoism, and self-centeredness, leads to non-fixated and non-grasping mindstates.

That is, non-grasping, non-clinging, non-attachment, and so forth are associated with the right view. The intermingling of attachment and grasping with jealousy, self-centeredness, egoism, resentment, bitterness, and so on—these are associated with the wrong view. In Buddhism then, in order to overcome fixation, we need to adopt the right view to counter the wrong view.

The wrong views we hold about ourselves, our mind, our emotions, and our desires, relate to how we ineffectively approach satisfying our desires. We habitually believe that if we could have more of what we desire, then those desires will be satisfied. That is seen as the wrong view. It is considered a wrong view as the attempt to satiate one's desires is what inflames them.

So there is a close relationship between wrong view, and grasping and fixation. Wrong view—*micchādiṭṭhi* (Pali) or *log par lta ba* in Tibetan—intensifies our sense of grasping onto things due to a semi-conscious belief in certainty. Through activities such as meditation and mindfulness[8] practice we can correct that wrong view and wrong approach. In order to correct that, we need to adopt the right view. The transcendental view is a concept that is associated with right view which then cultivates no view as one becomes free of any attachments.

There has been some confusion in Buddhism about the relationship between these three views: wrong view, right view, and no view, which is also known as the view of transcendence. There is a misconception and a confused idea held by some that in Buddhism from the outset we do not subscribe to any view and that all views lead to disturbance of the mind—that is, regardless of whether it is the wrong view or the right view that is being taken. The misconception is that Buddhists believe that both right view and wrong view lead to disturbance of the mind. This misunderstanding is based on the idea that transcendence of all views is the aim of Buddhism. If this belief is held, it creates a confusion regarding the meaning of right view, if the goal is understood to be the transcending of all views.

In Buddhism, we talk about abandoning wrong view, cultivation of right view, and also cultivation of no view or the transcendence of all views and often people associate this notion of transcendence of all views with Mahayana Buddhism but in early Buddhism, wrong view, right view, and transcendence of all views was present, even in the early Pali *suttas* such as the *Saṃyutta Nikāya*. It is important to understand, in relation to overcoming all fixation, that the three views are related. The transcendence of all views cannot be equated with the right view, or with the idea that wrong view is corrected by the right view. In Buddhism we see the transformation of views as a graduated or gradual path. It is more than an intellectual exercise where we try and swap one thought or view with another. We cannot simply change our thoughts, "OK, at first I've been thinking about these things and that is the wrong way to think. I can correct that by thinking something different or thinking that I just have to drop all kinds of views. I'll be free of all views and then I'll be free of all mental disturbances."

In early Buddhism, and later in Mahayana Buddhism, a graduated path to change is seen as part of meditational training. Through meditation, we first learn to recognize wrong view. We become conscious of the kinds of wrong views we subscribe to that have become unconsciously inculcated. We attempt to correct our thinking patterns to incorporate a more realistic view of reality, thus gradually developing the right view. Only then can we transcend even right view. Right view is eventually transcended as it is believed that it only gives us the partial truth.

In essence, wrong view does not reveal truth about the human condition. In Buddhism, what is true is not just propositional truth. What is true is measured in terms of our human experience. In particular, regarding views that perpetuate our samsaric existence, or alternatively, views that can progressively lead to liberation, it is considered that what is true leads to liberation and enlightenment and what is false leads to samsaric imprisonment. That which perpetuates our delusory mental states is considered the wrong view.

Truth in Relation to the Four Noble Truths

When we consider what is true and what is false it can be helpful to look at the concept of the Four Noble Truths[9]. They are not just a description of metaphysical truth or other propositional truths. The Four Noble Truths are about suffering, how to end suffering, and how to go about attaining the end of suffering. So first, we need to recognize and reflect upon suffering; then we look at the causes of suffering; we realize that the suffering can have an end point; and then we look at the approach of putting an end to suffering.

In Buddhism, what is false is what produces ignorance, what inflames negative forms of desire, and what inflames our anger, jealousy, envy, resentment, and other negative emotions. What is true is what cleans and purifies our mind, and what frees our mind of all forms of disturbances. So wrong view is associated with what we call *akusala*—akusala means "unwholesome mental states." The converse of that is called kusala "wholesome mental states." Right view then is associated with wholesome mental states and wrong view is associated with akusala, unwholesome mental states.

Once one has cultivated the right view, that of wholesome mental states, then one needs to transcend that as well. It is not the case that transcending all views is the antidote to wrong view. The antidote to wrong view is right view and the antidote to right view is the transcendence of all views. It is a gradual weaning-off from these habitual tendencies related to view. What is referred to here is different degrees of fixation. There is a tremendous level of fixation involved with wrong view—that is, we have deep and strong attachment to our views. We cherish our strongly held views and belief. This can be corrected by the cultivation of right view, *sammādiṭṭhi*, to reduce or lessen our level of fixation. So, right view is connected to a more subtle form of fixation. This subtle fixation can then be overcome through the notion of the transcendence of all views.

The Difference between Intellectual Understanding and Direct Experience

In Buddhism, through not understanding how the world arises and ceases—the impermanent and insubstantial nature of all things—we develop wrong view. When we develop an understanding of dependent arising[10], which is how the world arises and ceases, we can establish the right view. That means we overcome the dense fixation on our preciously held belief systems and the unconscious expectation of certainty and permanency. This freeing up of the mind brings an increase in mental dexterity, and is thus an antidote to the fixated state of wrong view. This puts us in a much better position to then release any remaining fixation. We are in a better position to go beyond the theory of dependent arising and are able to realize the transcendence of all views.

We are making a distinction here between how we intellectually understand the way the world works and how we can experience the world directly in a non-deluded and non-tainted way. Dharma knowledge or understanding how the world works is not the same as having the experience of how the world works. As long as there is a perspective on how we are seeing what we experience, we are looking at it from a deluded or tainted, impure position. When we experience directly how the world arises and dissipates, there is no need for *pratītyasamutpāda* or the dependent arising viewpoint.

Once this insight has been gained, one experiences dependent arising instead of experiencing the world through the filter of our delusional mind. The delusory mind does not allow us to see things as they are. We see the world based on our belief systems and so react to things in a delusional way. We grasp onto things to create more certainty and permanence due to an innate resistance to seeing things as arising and ceasing. We do not want to see the arising and cessation of the world. We grasp and cling to how we interpret our experiences to protect us from experiencing untainted reality.

We do not normally see or experience the spontaneous arising and dissipation directly on a moment by moment basis. So we first cultivate this worldview to learn to see the world and our experience in that way. Even if we do not experience the world in that way, we incorporate the view of dependent arising to help us see the world in that way. By making an effort to see the impermanence in the world, we begin to experience it as well. Due to a shift in the mind, we look at our experience differently. By looking at the world in a different way, we begin to experience the world differently as well.

We eventually need to transcend all views because even right view can be latched onto and we can become fixated on it. With right view there are degrees of fixation, from gross to more subtle.

In relation to our personal fixations, even without talking about philosophy or having explicit notions about metaphysics, we implicitly hold onto certain ideas about our identity.

Normally, we are fixated with the notion of the self, identity, and difference or separateness. Without having necessarily done any explicit philosophical reflections, we have certain ideas and beliefs about "who we are" and we develop fixation and certainty around "who we are." For example, if we look at ourselves, our body, brain, senses, and mind, we may conclude that the notion of the self that I have is nothing other than my body-mind complex. In this instance we are thinking the self is the same as the body and mind complex. Furthermore, we may have a different belief or view of the self. We may think the self is something different from the body-mind complex, that the self possesses the body, and the self possesses the mind. This belief sees the body-mind complex as different or separate from the self.

These examples illustrate the types of fixation on identity that can be strongly held. To support such positions we can get caught up with conceptual formulations such as affirmation or negation. If we say that self and body or self and mind are the same, we are affirming their identity. If we say they are different, we are negating their identity.

From the Buddhist point of view, all fixations are developed from these binary concepts of either/or, and either the same or different. Our thought patterns support and uphold our conceptual formulations through affirmation and negation. These thought patterns cause fixation—that is, we fixate on the notion of oneness or lack of difference or separation; or we fixate on the notion of separation and difference.

From the Buddhist point of view, conceptual formulation based on affirmation and negation is not an intellectual exercise alone;

strongly held beliefs and thought patterns evoke emotional and other habitualized responses.

When we affirm or negate the identity of certain things as identical or different, we generate strong attachment to our position. Strong attachment to a particular position produces strong feelings. We tend to defend and support our positions, desperately latching onto those ideas. We find there is a lot of emotional investment involved in maintaining our conceptual positions based on our views, beliefs, and opinions.

From the Buddhist perspective, we correct these fixations by adopting the right view of insubstantiality and interconnectedness. Right view challenges the idea of certainty in the conclusions we support about things being the same or different. It challenges the idea of seeing things in a definite form as being either one way or the other. In terms of dependent arising we do not have to think of things as either being definitely identical or having a definite difference. In that way our fixation on thinking that things are either the same or different will lessen. If that fixation lessens, our emotional investment and responses will also reduce and the mental agitation will begin to subside.

Seeing things as dependently arising goes beyond affirmation and negation. If affirming, we may see that there is an immutable fixed reality to all we see and experience, and a physical reality that we encounter on a daily basis. With negation, we may say that there is nothing, that everything is fabricated by the mind, that there is no reality to anything that we experience, and all our experiences are *māyā*, an illusion. From the position of right view, we avoid these two extremes: the extreme of affirming that there is some kind of fixed immutable reality that we are encountering and being fixated upon; and the alternative view of thinking that everything we experience is illusory, in a real and literal sense and that our experiences are like dreams.

From a Buddhist point of view, getting fixated on either of these extremes is wrong view. Right view or dependent arising allows us to see the world for what it is. It is real enough but the world does not present itself in the way that we think it does. The world cannot be experienced outside our mind, because we can only experience the world using our mind. We can say the world exists but our apprehension of it is not objective. It is subjective; it is subject to our perspective and how we apprehend and experience the world. It does not exist of its own accord, as we experience it. The world arises in relation to our self, in relation to the subject who has these experiences. Natural phenomena arise in the world due to causes and conditions. When the right causes and conditions come together, it allows certain things to arise.

Understanding that all manifestations, physical or otherwise, are produced due to causes and conditions is a great antidote to fixation. "Fixation" means we get fixated on the singularity of things—that is, we single out particular characteristics and then get fixated on that. If we realize that things are conditionally produced, we cannot get too fixated on anything because whatever we experience, whatever arises, has arisen as part of a network of interconnecting events. Our mind or our senses, immediately, out of habit, may select an object and focus on that aspect as the subject of our fixation. In reality, what we have fixated on is only one manifestation of many interconnecting fields and events that are simultaneously occurring at that very moment. Another person witnessing the same event may notice a different aspect of the experience and latch onto a different aspect as the subject of fixation. Thus the same event can be apprehended and experienced very differently by those sharing the experience. The world is much more complex and varied than our mind is usually capable of processing. When we recognize that, we realize that the world is multifarious and multifaceted. There are many interconnecting events and fields arising at any given time. Not only that, but whatever has arisen does not stay, is not stable, so what we have seen and become fixated upon may have disappeared. However, our fixation may still remain intact or even become stronger.

Chapter 5
Developing a Liberated Perspective

Intellectually, the discursive mind engages with certain things. We are thinking most of the time, and we all have some favorite topics that we think about and return to again and again. This is true visually and audially as well. Immediately, out of habit, we notice certain things more than others. What catches our attention repeatedly may not be noticed by another person.

These favorite things continually catch our attention and thus impact and affect our mind, emotional life, self-perception, and sense of self-identity. By recognizing these attractions and thought patterns, we can gradually learn to relinquish our fixation on the wrong view—that is, we can relinquish the idea that our experiences and perspectives are entirely real. Thus, with the wrong view we see things in isolation and as stand-alone truths and entities with great certainty. With wrong view we see things either in terms of affirmation or negation: identity, where we identify affirmatively with the object; or difference, where we do not identify with the object, and negate or are at odds with the object.

We may gradually develop this ability to see things in relation to *dependent arising*. Dependent arising recognizes that things do not arise independently but depend on appropriate causes and conditions for their manifestation. As everything is dependent on causes and conditions, their form will not ultimately endure as causes and conditions change. This can be understood intellectually. To loosen our beliefs in our personalized reality we can apply the notion of dependent arising to our experiences. As we become acquainted with that, then gradually we may experience the dependent arising within ourselves. So we may experience the insubstantial nature of all things, also referred to in Buddhism as "emptiness" or "being empty of inherent existence." The way it is expressed in Buddhism is that first we have to have dharma knowledge—that is, knowledge of dependent arising. The knowledge does not just remain as knowledge because, in Buddhism, attachment to that knowledge itself is seen as a form of delusion. As long as there is some remaining attachment to the knowledge as a static solid truth, there is still delusion, there is still mental fixation to be overcome.

If we experience dependent arising in terms of our thoughts, emotions, feelings, and perception—how we see, feel, interact with others, behave towards our environment and other individuals—and do this with the realization of dependent arising, we have then transcended view. If we can experience the world in that way, there is no need for view. We do not need the perspective that sees things in a particular way. We only need the perspective to see things in a particular way when our habits are particularly strong. When our habits are well-entrenched due to our experience of attraction and aversion, likes and dislikes, our strong feelings of pain and pleasure, then we need to develop a new perspective in order to loosen the hold the habitual tendencies have upon us. In order to overcome well-entrenched tendencies and habits, we need to adopt the right view of dependent arising.

When we have the experience of dependent arising, the transcendence of views follows on from adopting the right view. However, the right view and the transcendent view are not seen as the same.

Some modern Buddhist scholars have even written articles about how one can transcend the view and yet hold a view, the right view.

If we believe right view is the transcendence of all views, then the transcendence of all views cannot be the transcendence of all views because it is the right view. To understand the relationship between the transcendence of all views and right view or correct view, sammādiṭṭhi in Pali, is to understand the progressive and gradual way we can skillfully work with our minds to genuinely create change. We progressively use the perspective of or belief in dependent arising to enable realization of the nature of reality. It is important to recognize that right view is not the final position. Realization in Buddhism is not the realization of correct view, as such. It is the transcendence of all views. We utilize sammādiṭṭhi, right view, in order to reach that level, in order to reach the state of no view. In that respect then, right view has a vital and important place in one's spiritual journey and attainments.

Right view has to do with *right understanding*. Right understanding refers to the importance of our understanding corresponding with how things actually are. How things are is not about an objective reality, something out there that is separate from us. What we are trying to understand is not detached from our subjectivity. It is not seen as an objectively distant, transcendent reality we are trying to get a grip on. The reality that we want to gain some understanding of is intimately tied to our subjectivity. Therefore, the knowledge gained is not detached but intimate and that knowledge has a transformative impact. The knowledge transforms our consciousness. There is a revolution in our consciousness. Our consciousness goes through a significant shift because of the knowledge gained.

Therefore, right view is both descriptive and prescriptive. By cultivating right view we transform ourselves through developing that knowledge, the knowledge of *dharma*. Dharmas means "all dependently arising phenomena." Mental and physical phenomena are called "dharmas" in Buddhism. By having that knowledge, not getting fixated on any one dharma but realizing the many dharmas—the interconnecting events and fields are called "dharmas"—that understanding, in itself, is transformative[11].

When change or transformation in our perception occurs, we realize and experience dependent arising. When we experience dependent arising, we do not need the aid of right view. We do not need that perspective any more as we do not need to remind ourselves to hold that perspective. This perspective is called *Middle View*, both in Mahayana Buddhism and in early Buddhism. The reason it is called "middle view" is because it refuses to lend significance to either one of the binary concepts, identity or difference, by saying "it is like this" or "it is not like that"; or "it is the same" or "it is different."

When we see things as dependent arising, it is important not to fall into the extreme of saying nothing exists, or saying that there are individual things out there that we encounter. That individualization is how we apprehend things normally. We normally perceive things as separate and having separated them they become objects of our fixation. So the other extreme is seeing and believing our fixated perspective is how things truly exist.

The middle view helps us to avoid falling into the two extreme views of nihilism or eternalism, which means to have the correct or right view. By having that correct view, our fixation will diminish. As discussed, when there is less fixation, we will be grasping and clinging onto things less as we will have developed a fairly good understanding of the dynamism and interconnection of the world, and our experience of the world will correspond to this understanding.

The middle view allows us to appreciate this dynamism, and engage in and enjoy the world more directly, realizing how things are, in a less tainted way. *How things are* does not mean how things exist in some kind of static form. *Yathābhūtaṃ.* "How things are"—

gnas lugs in Tibetan—or "how things exist," does not mean getting metaphysical insight into how things exist in some kind of fixed way. "How things are," means how things continually arise and cease, arise and cease. It refers to the dynamic nature of the world.

If we understand that, then we realize that ultimately there is nothing to get fixated on because of the dynamic quality of the world, and our potentially dynamic experience of that world. We can have a stable viewpoint about different subjective experiences of the world. Nevertheless, we can still recognize that there is nothing to get fixated on. From a Buddhist point of view, for practical purposes our views about many things are often adopted from others and the environment we live in and that allows us to understand many things in a consistent and particular way. This is necessary on the relative day-to-day level. From the ultimate perspective there is nothing to get fixated on.

So while acknowledging the importance of some stability in our perspectives and views, we can still maintain an understanding of the importance of distinguishing between wrong view and right view. The idea of transcending all views does not mean there is no difference between right and wrong view, as has been expressed by some. Rather, on the conventional level, we need to see wrong view as being our strong tendency to see the world as fixed. The right view, unlike what we might normally think, means "view without dogma and intolerance."

The middle view encompasses different viewpoints and philosophical positions. These are tolerated, and some may even be accepted, as an expression of the middle view. There may also be differences in how the middle view is expressed in different contexts. The middle view can be expressed in social or economic terms, in relation to the environment, or in terms of ethics, and so on. The middle view can be expressed in many contexts, not just within Buddhist teachings. This same conclusion has been drawn by many scholars. The middle view does not adopt a single theoretical position whereby everything else is seen as false.

In summary, we first learn to distinguish the wrong view from the right view. Secondly, we adopt the right view. Over time, with consideration and contemplation, we realize that right view is not a narrow view but a view that encompasses a number of alternate positions on varieties of issues. Understanding this posits right view as the middle view.

That is considered to be the case on the conventional level. Ultimately, one needs to experience the breadth of openness and tolerance within the middle view. It is not sufficient to just have an understanding of the middle view. Even though the middle view has the potential to transform us, nevertheless, any view is not sufficient to transform us completely. To really become liberated, not just to be transformed to a certain limited level, one needs to overcome fixation on the middle view as well.

Someone who has transcended all views, realized dependent arising, and knowledge of the dharma phenomena may still make use of the correct view on the relative level in order to discourse with others and be engaged in the world.

We may think that if someone realizes the state that transcends all views, that the individual has no use for any kind of viewpoint. It is true the person may not have any need for views but in order to communicate, in order to engage with the world, one would still have to approach it via sammādiṭṭhi, via the right view. So on the conventional level the liberated person may still make use of right view.

In Buddhism, overcoming fixation is part of overcoming grasping and clinging, as we have been discussing. Real grasping and clinging can be overcome only if we let go of fixation. We can only let go of fixation completely and totally when we attain the transcendental state of no view. By deepening our understanding of the wrong and right view, we gradually attain the transcendental state of no view. When we attain that state, we have let go of all forms of grasping and fixation.

What we call "realization" is not about understanding the view; it is about embodying the reality purported by the view. What is meant by *insight into reality*, or *gaining knowledge into reality*, is that one comes to embody that very reality that one has developed some understanding of, so there ceases to be any separation between the idea and the experience.

If we really see things as dependent arising, our tendency to get fixated will become lessened and we will be more directly engaged with the world, so then we have the experience of the middle view. The wrong view means we continually become fixated, desperately latching onto things and beliefs. In so doing we can become oblivious of almost everything else. That is contrary to the concept of dependent arising. When we hold wrong view, if something pops up and draws our attention, we can become completely locked into it and our fixation then becomes our reality.

If we see and experience dependent arising, even if we focus our mind on specific features of the world, we retain a broader understanding so that what we are focusing on does not become separated out. We experience the connectedness of that which has our focus.

It is incorrect to think that if we meditate, we will attain non-view so then we do not have to worry about understanding right view. Rather, within our meditation we should try to develop the right view. Right view has nothing to do with dogma, commandments in holy books, or anything of that kind. It is about understanding ourselves and understanding dependent arising or the notion of emptiness, as it is referred to in Mahayana Buddhism. In Buddhism we speak about using the Buddhist view as a vehicle or boat to cross the turbulent waters of samsara and once one has crossed the turbulent waters, one leaves the boat on the shore; we do not have to carry the boat with us. In a similar way, you use the *Dharmic* view to get to the other shore, the other shore being nirvana or enlightenment. Once we have attained nirvana, we do not need right view because one embodies that view. Once we have established a more enlightened perspective of how to view things by adopting the right view, we can then leave it behind.

Fundamentally, "dependent arising" means that the mind and the material world do not arise independently of one another. We emphasize the mind because we experience the world through the mind. That is the only way we can experience the world. We cannot step outside our mind and experience the world. That does not mean only the mind exists. Rather, it means we apprehend and experience the world in a particular way because of the kind of mind we have. This includes the influence of our beliefs, dispositions, and habitual tendencies on how we see and experience the world generally.

Mind Only School

The Yogācāra School or the *Mind only school* may say that there is no objective material world external to the mind. However that does not mean they are referring to subjective idealism *per se*[12]. What is being referred to is the idea of collective karma—that is, different groups of sentient beings, due to inheriting similar karmic conditions, develop similar perceptions of the world. So humans experience this human world similarly. Animals, insects, and other such sentient beings experience the world differently from human beings, due to different sensory apparatuses, levels of consciousness, and differing conditions generally, thus they bear different sets of karmic imprints. Therefore they are inscribed differently.

In that sense, the mind only school is not saying that this world is created by your individual mind, or that people you meet and interact with, as well as the material world, are all just part of your own mind. This has also been said generally about subjective idealism anyway. Buddhist idealists do not go that far either. They believe in the idea of a common experience and a common world that is not unique to just one particular individual's experience. Some from the mind only school may have indicated that there is nothing beyond that common experience of the material world, beyond the shared karmic vision of that world.

However, many commentators have claimed that if we look at the original works of the founders of the mind only school, that interpretation is a misunderstanding. It has been suggested that they were actually saying that the only experience we can have of any aspect of the world is limited by the mind and that is all there is. That is why it is called "mind only." So the distinction there between the different interpretations is suggesting that the mind only school did not believe there is nothing there and that only mind exists. But rather, they were saying that beyond the mind, we can only guess what reality there might be. It is not saying that there is no reality at all.

As discussed, in order to work with our fixation, we need to try to deal with wrong view, right view, and no view. This corresponds with how our *kleśas*, our emotional conflicts, are spoken of. For example, in Buddhism you will often hear the idea about abandoning negative emotions and cultivating positive emotions and eventually we even stop cultivating positive emotions. I think it is important to clarify here that we do not try to abandon negative emotions as such. By cultivating positive emotions, we reduce the impact and eventually overcome negative emotions, or render them benign. The same thing is said regarding karma: first we have to learn to create positive karma in order to overcome negative karma, and then we can even stop creating positive karma.

It is important to understand that, particularly in Mahayana Buddhism, this is a very common typology of the Buddhist path—

that is to say, you start wherever you are and then you move through.

It is important to appreciate the idea of progressing through stages. Otherwise we may become fixated on one issue and not realize the fuller context. It is easy for some people to feel that right from the beginning we should try to transcend all views through the practice of meditation. Similar expectations are often expressed about overcoming karma but overcoming fixation, grasping, or even karma is not as simple as just deciding to. The semi-conscious habitual patterns can be very strong and may have persisted for many years.

We first need to begin to erode our negative habits by utilizing a counter-force. Once we have progressed and reduced the effect of a bad habit, we then need to relinquish our fixation on the methods used to help with such a transformation. The antidote has worked and we then need to relinquish that particular approach in order to continue to progress on the path.

To reiterate, negative habits are overcome by positive habits and then we learn to go even beyond positive habits. Going beyond positive habits does not mean we are not discriminating between negative habits and positive habits. We may use discriminating awareness which means that we may still discriminate but we discriminate with non-attachment and non-fixation. Our discriminatory awareness is born out of insight and not out of prejudice, bias, and mental fixation. From the Buddhist point of view, we will always need to make decisions, and we make them based on our desire. There is nothing wrong with that. The main thing is not to get caught up with too much indecision. We do not need to become too anxious or worried or allow all kinds of disturbing emotions to arise based on our decisions.

According to Buddhism, if we allow our grasping nature to get the better of us, it always causes problems, disturbing our ability to see things clearly and thus clouding our decisions. Basically, at the beginning, when working with our disturbing habitual tendencies, it is not easy to not grasp or cling onto things. It is a matter of degree, so we begin by easing up on our worry and becoming less bogged down by the weight of whatever decision has been made.

In Buddhism, we are taught to be serious about the world and how we conduct ourselves within it. At the same time, we are encouraged to be light-hearted and not take ourselves too seriously. We need to find a balance between taking the world seriously and viewing our misapprehension of the world with light-hearted humor. Taking everything too seriously can be wearing. It can create too much grasping, too much neediness, and fixation on how we believe things should be. It can become exhausting and we can become bogged down by all our expectations.

Light-heartedness keeps us more cheerful, up-beat, and stops us obsessing about things too much. I think sometimes Buddhists may want to try the impossible. Instead of trying the impossible, we need to stick to what is possible and focus on what we can do to work on ourselves in a realistic and gradual manner. Instead of trying not to desire at all the things that we desire, we can instead just desire them and watch the activity of our minds within the desiring process without getting too bogged down or too serious. Building self-knowledge in that way, over time, helps us get a handle on what is going on in our minds. Through our desires we can motivate and propel ourselves towards a more uplifted reality and experience. Sometimes in our enthusiasm we may want to renounce everything and retire to the Himalayas and live in a cave. But, practically speaking, it might be more profitable to deal with what we can do, what we can work on, and not fantasize about what is less likely to be happening.

Chapter 6
Rationality and Conviction

I suggest that Buddhism has said more about desire than any of the other religious traditions that I am aware of. This is not a value judgment and I am not suggesting that Buddhism is superior to other forms of religion. Rather, in terms of this subject matter, Buddhism has had a lot to say about desire and how we should go about managing it.

The popular image might be that you go to Thailand, Burma, or Tibet and see monks and nuns as renunciants who have renounced many worldly things. We may consider that they have worked on their desire and therefore they have no more dealings with the world. This understanding of Buddhism and what it means to be a renunciant monk or nun is mistaken. It has more to do with developing a positive attitude towards desire in order to engage in the world more effectively, than wanting to have no more dealings with the world.

If we look at desire from a western philosophical point of view, from Plato through to Kant, you will not see desire given a significant role for in-depth discussion. Rather, you will see everything that is distasteful about human beings traced back to the fact that we have desire. Having desire is somehow related to our bodily, carnal nature, according to much of western philosophy, and there is nothing redemptive—in Buddhist terms, nothing "liberating"—that will come out of it. Therefore it is often concluded within the many western traditions that reason and rationality is what human beings should aim towards and excel in, to overcome our desires.

I believe, for Plato and others, that reason was seen as a distinct faculty. From this perspective it is not just that we have the capacity to think clearly and think things through, in some kind of maze of conceptual difficulty, but we have a rational faculty as well. This capacity of rationality, in simplified terms, is seen by many such philosophers as distinct from our carnal, physical, and animalistic nature.

It appears that the notion of desire has not been accommodated very well in the western way of thinking. Until the time of British empiricists such as Hume, the majority of western thinkers did not accord any kind of importance to the role of desire, in relation to morality or ethics. It was believed that acting morally was not about what you desired but more about whether you were thinking in a rational or irrational fashion. If you behave irrationally, then you behave in an immoral way which means you have yielded to your desires and urges and thus have become immoral. If you want to be moral, you have to be very rational, very clear-minded, and not expressive, keeping your emotions within bounds. That emotionality should be kept private and contained.

Within much of theological discourse, this belief was endemic, the belief that it is paramount to keep the beast that is within us contained. If we allow the beast to come out, it will go on a rampage and we will become sinful and be condemned.

It has been very clear that in the west, in terms of western philosophy, theology, and some other disciplines, there was some resistance demonstrated in relation to accommodating various forms of desire. Desires were normally seen as anathema to our rational potential and human beings should strive towards becoming more rational, logical, and clear-thinking. In Christianity, faith may often take the place of rationality when it comes to containing one's desires. Be it faith or reason, with either one there was considered to be no room for desire. Desire was to be denigrated, and relegated to the outer parameters of our main concerns, those being the cultivation of either reason or faith.

Conversely, Hume stated that reason would need to play a secondary role to desire. Hume made room for desire, even in terms of our moral aspirations. He was quite in favor of the notion of being able to accommodate human feelings and emotions, including desire. For that reason, Hume's propositions were uncommon. Further along we have Friedrich Nietzsche, and Nietzsche and some post–modernists, while their theories do take a different route, nonetheless they emphasized the importance of desire and human emotions.

In the west it has commonly been that there is some kind of war going on between people who emphasize the importance of human emotions, including desire, and people who do not wish to discuss, review, or acknowledge it. There has been a strong emphasis on distinguishing animals from human beings. The distinguishing characteristics reside in the ability to have faith in God and be able to exercise our rational capacity. In contrast, animals can be seen as expressing certain forms of emotion such as aggression, the desire to copulate, eat food, and so on.

On a side note, I wish to express that I personally have a lot of respect for other religious traditions and I do not want to say anything derogatory about theism or Christianity. Many early philosophers and theologians would suggest that our rational capacity is put there by God. My point is, not that the Buddhist position is better or worse, but rather, that in Buddhism we believe that our rational capacity and our emotional inclinations coincide. If we look at Buddha's own discourses, we can see that the Buddha did not say we should only think clearly. The Buddha did say however that we should reason well in order to overcome certain forms of desire. What the Buddha said was that we should reason well and exercise awareness and mindfulness together.

The way to overcome desire, a method which was present right from the beginning in Buddhism, was not about saying categorically that all desire is bad, or that we need to develop other forms of mental faculty, whether faith or reason, in order to transcend our desirous nature. Rather, the way to overcome desire was to distinguish different forms and strengths of desire. Through developing this type of discernment, one can recognize forms of desire that can be disruptive and forms of desire that are not disruptive. That was what the Buddha was more concerned about.

In Buddhism there is a place for reason, which may not be emphasized enough in western Buddhism. There can often be a lot of emphasis given to the practice of mindfulness and awareness and related practices. The Buddha was very concerned with how to think clearly because clear-mindedness is so helpful when our desires become overwhelming. In these instances we can tend to automatically indulge in a sloppy type of thinking. Due to our fantasies, expectations, wishes, and unrealizable goals, we can become ungrounded and begin to believe our deluded and chaotic thinking makes sense. Our capacity to think "so rationally" becomes preponderant over other considerations.

What is different about Buddhism when compared to other philosophies and religious traditions, is that in Buddhism, faith, reason, and the practice of mindfulness-awareness are all emphasized together. When these come together, we are better able to deal with different forms of desire. There is not one single thing that is called "desire" which would automatically make us become sinful. We are not simply talking about sexual desire or the physical desire for food because of hunger or for drink because of thirst, but about all kinds of desire, including the desire for security, to extend life, to end life, and so on.

As I have presented it here, the ubiquitous nature of desire is addressed in Buddhism. There is no simplification within the philosophical theory but, rather, the many forms of desire that we experience are dealt with. How to overcome desire is discussed in terms of how it can be reduced and ultimately overcome by exercising our rational capacity and with conviction or faith in the teachings. Because we are normally unaware or ignorant of our state, we cannot easily decipher what is good for us and what is not good for us. So advice is made available through the teachings to clarify one's situation and relationship with desire.

To address such an issue, it may be well-advised to listen to the Buddha, or other masters such as Nagarjuna, Chandrakirti, the Dalai Lama, and so on. In that way we can review our approach, beliefs, and attitudes and really begin to address our issues more fully. Not everything that we experience or can reason about is going to bring about change so listening to or reading about the men and women masters within Buddhism can provide tremendous insight and support.

In Buddhism, we recognize the need for both faith and reason to coincide to effect change. In terms of faith or conviction, to believe in something such as a traditional, well-grounded theory or philosophy, can provide us with insight beyond what we have experienced in our own lives. This additional insight and explanation of the human condition generally, can help to provide an understanding that aids in transforming our lives. Unfortunately, it can be too limiting to rely only on what we have experienced. Some people may believe that one can only believe what one has experienced. The idea that you can only know what you experience is supported by some fairly extreme empiricists such as Rudolf Carnap of the Vienna Circle. Such philosophers were known as logical positivists[13]. In Buddhism the idea that you can only believe in what you see or experience is seen as limiting and unworkable, when seeking to understand how the mind works, in order to directly overcome some types of suffering.

Buddhism emphasizes that in order to understand what we are working with in our current karmic situation and to change and reduce our suffering, we need to understand more fully our condition. To gain this understanding, we need to access three capacities. We need to access our own experience, in conjunction with reason or rationality, and faith or conviction. All three elements—experience, rationality, and conviction—are important for growth and transformation. The interplay of these three elements allows us to be able to more acutely distinguish the desires that will aid us and make us flourish; and those desires that will keep us entrapped in the samsaric world.

Buddhism emphasizes that experience is important but we should not over-emphasize experience at the expense of rationality and conviction. We cannot simply meditate sitting on a cushion hoping things will become clear. Studying the teachings to build conviction and understanding and using the mind's rational capacities, in combination, provides far greater clarity.

The Buddhist view is that experience has to be validated. We can have all kinds of experiences. How do we validate which of our experiences are helpful and genuine and which are superficial, though experienced as very real? The practice of mindfulness may provide some clarity as previously discussed. Just having the experience and being present as much as possible may not be enough either. The question remains, how do we distinguish something that is illusory from a more genuine experience? If we have not yet had realization, we also need to use rationality and faith to make that distinction clearer.

Realization is the goal but the question remains, how do we get there? How do we have the realization? We have the realization by first having an experience and then measuring that experience, assessing it in the following way by asking pertinent questions to clarify one's thoughts. Does it make sense? Am I really deluding myself through creating fictional stories to support my version of reality or is this real? These types of questions are clarified by returning to the literature of the great female and male masters of the tradition. We need to see if our experience and thoughts fundamentally make sense, not just to ourselves but also more broadly.

So we have the experience and then we have to try to make sense of it. Even after observing the experience mindfully to see it for what it is, we may still remain unconvinced and have doubts. We then need to initiate our faith, which is a real conviction in the teachings of the Dharma that explain how we grasp and fixate and so on. If we persist in this endeavor, reviewing our experience mindfully, with rationality and conviction, our experiences can be transformed. These experiences can become radically different from the experiences that we have when we are not cultivating mindfulness and awareness.

Traditionally, we carry out our reasoning exercises in relation to Buddhist epistemology. That is, we reason about experience both in terms of what we can directly see, our direct perception, and what we do not directly perceive but can actually make a good inference of.

For example, if we see something visually, then there is sensory evidence of what is going on. If you believe it is raining outside and somebody else believes it is not raining, then one can verify that by checking outside to see if it is raining or not. You check, using your senses. This is called "direct perception"—*tshad ma* in Tibetan.

There are other experiences that we directly see and perceive but our conclusions from those are inferred. For example, one might believe karma exists because whenever you have good thoughts, positive mental states, and so forth, that leads to a happy state of mind, be it enduring or temporary. When you are feeling positive, one can infer that these kinds of experiences are generated from positive thoughts and positive mental attitudes. So when one is feeling good, that general sense of well-being is then related to one's experience of having positive thoughts.

Taking inference a step further, if you continue to engage in having positive thoughts and positive mental attitudes and believe that that will facilitate a better rebirth, you have made a connective leap. From being positive and, as Nietzsche would say, having a "yea-saying" attitude towards life rather than a "nay-saying" attitude—that is, having a life-affirming attitude: you are alive, you feel good—to expect that to cause you to have a positive rebirth in the next life as well, you have to make an inference.

In Buddhism we often make those kinds of inferences which require faith or conviction, because conviction is based on logical inference. Conviction should not be completely divorced from reason and rationality. Conviction is based on reasoning but it is reasoning based on inference. Reasoning based on inference is seen as the foundation of faith or conviction. Therefore, we believe in the testimony of reliable sources such as the Dalai Lama and other great masters as an invaluable part of how we cultivate knowledge. That approach is valuable for whatever it is that we want to know more about.

Even as an academic, if you were seeking to study history in great detail, you would likely research and reference those considered to be the most reliable historians, rather than choosing sources less specialized, less knowledgeable, and exhibiting strong biases. So one would review and value the historians' accounts of the period in history they have presented. Those historians have made inferences from the information they have available to provide an account of those times. You really have no way of knowing fully someone's bias and the effect their bias has on their historical account. So one reviews the information from a variety of reliable sources and from there makes an inference.

In this way, we accumulate knowledge. We accumulate knowledge based on the trust we have in the source; we develop faith and conviction in those most knowledgeable. We believe in certain historians to tell us the story closest to the truth as best they can. As post-modernism will point out, we need to take into account the cultural milieu that the historian lived in to create the proper context for their description of history. From a Buddhist perspective also, contextualizing information is important. This approach helps to unhinge our tendency to fixate. Rather than thinking "this is how it is," one contextualizes it to promote a wider view. This approach in many ways is comparable to the middle view spoken about earlier.

Thus it is explained that experience, reason or rationality, and faith or conviction combine together to empower us to transform ourselves. This assists us to deal with our various forms of desire. In Buddhist traditions it really comes back to desire, always. Buddhism does not dwell too much on hatred or other forms of negative emotion. Buddhism is always talking about different forms of desire, always.

From that, we may then draw the conclusion that in Buddhism the recognition of the diversity of desire is fully acknowledged. The responsibility of a Buddhist then is learning how to transform the desires that we have, be they positive or negative. How do we make these judgments to utilize different forms of desire to advance ourselves? How do we both recognize and manage negative forms of desire that are self-destructive? While we are learning from our experiences, developing rational consideration and listening to and contemplating the teachings of the Buddha and other great masters, our desires are transforming. In Buddhism, understanding about desire is already about the transformation of desire. We should not make a distinction between theoretical understanding and learning how to transform desire. The theoretical understanding of desire is part of the practical implementation of transforming desire.

This is a unique aspect of Buddhism in that we do not make a distinction between theory and practice. Theory is always about practice and vice versa. If you want to practice this or that, you have to have the theory behind it to support the practice. If you have a certain theory, you have to know how to implement that theory. It is not something abstract, something divorced from life experiences. It is part of life's experience.

Human beings are desirous creatures and our realm—"realm" being a term that can also describe our psychological disposition— is known as *kāmadhātu*. *Kāma* means "desire" and covers many forms of desire, so is used more broadly; *dhātu* means "realm." So kāmadhātu means "realm of desire"—that is to say, we live psychophysically in kāmadhātu.

It maybe worthwhile noting that, kāma is not "karma" and *kāmasutra* is not the same as karmasutra. Kāmasutra is the sutra of desire but it is important to note that kāmasutra is not just about sex but more broadly about sensuality and so on. Thus, in that way, kāmasutra and kāmadhatu have the same meaning. "Kāmadhātu," as mentioned earlier, is used to indicate desire in its many different forms, whereas the word *rāga*, for example, which also means "desire," is less broad and more focused on a particular form of desire.

Rāga can be contrasted with *dveṣa*, which refers to more negative forms of desire such as anger, jealousy, resentment, and so on. We may get angry because we do not get what we want, what we desire; we expect something from somebody and that person is not forthcoming so we are disappointed, we can feel let down. These are our tendencies.

Working with Desire as a Meditation Practice

In Buddhism, because we recognize the diverse and ubiquitous nature of desire, different Buddhist schools have come up with varieties of practices and ways of dealing with desire that encompass a wide range of human experience. We are instructed to deal with desire in different ways. There is not one unique way that we deal with the different responses to desire and habitual tendencies.

Within the diversity, however, there is some kind of underlying current that is common and pervasive, which is to do with the grasping, clinging, and fixation.

It does not matter whether we are following the exoteric forms of Buddhism or the esoteric forms of Buddhism. Even if we are discussing Tantricism, it is still about overcoming excessive grasping, clinging, and fixation. That is the underlying theme. So in Buddhism it does not matter what we are talking about in relation to desire. As long as we have grasping and clinging, and continue to fixate on specific things, we are somewhat lost and limited. If we were not caught up with so much grasping and fixation, we would be free to experience different forms of desire, and could even make use of these experiences in a constructive fashion.

Approaching Desire through Renunciation

Recognizing and contrasting negative and positive forms of desire within the mind is extremely important. In certain Buddhist contexts the concept of renunciation is emphasized. In the case of desire, we need to renounce certain things to avoid experiencing the corresponding negative forms of desire. For example, in Buddhism one may become a monastic to avoid or reduce distractions and irritants that can throw one's concentration and move one into a state of agitation. That individual then is given the opportunity to practice mindfulness and awareness, to use reason to understand what is fuelling desire, and to develop faith and conviction.

A reasonable question to ask regarding renunciation is why does Buddhism—particularly in early Buddhism—emphasize renunciation? It may be very easy for us to think of early Buddhism as being not so very different from the approach we have discussed from western philosophy and Christian theology. We may even think of equating Buddhism with the Augustinian form of

Christian theology, for example. St. Augustine, having been converted to Christianity, seemed to have considered the body itself as somewhat evil, thought of the world as the Devil's playground, and considered that everything that we see, smell, taste, and touch is the Devil's clever trick to take us away or lead us astray from God. This is, of course, not a proper representation of Christianity. I use this example more to point out that some religious traditions can be scathing about certain forms of desire. Some approaches to renunciation can be equated with that type of approach.

In fact, renunciation in Buddhism is approached quite differently. One becomes a renunciant or monastic not because the world itself is evil or that there is a monotheistic ruler governing the world. Rather, renunciation is designed to reduce distractions. It is also essential in this and all situations to measure and check one's desires. Unchecked desires can go haywire and bring ruin to us. Therefore, if thought necessary, the renunciant sees that aspect of training is extremely important to address, and they can best address it in a monastic environment.

The Buddha himself said being a renunciant or a monastic was desirable but he did not say being a monk or nun was the only option available to somebody to become spiritually advanced. The person who is spiritually advanced, who attains the ultimate goal of spiritual attainment, is called an "arahant." In the Buddha's early suttas you will find several arahants mentioned; some were monastics and some were laity.

From the beginning of Buddhism there was the idea—which has become somewhat lost—that the *bhikkhu* or *bhikkhunī*, the ordained male or female member of the sangha, was the ideal that one could aspire to. If we consider early times in Asia with extended families, where grandparents, parents, aunts and uncles, everybody lived together, for the spiritually minded, the opportunity for meditation, study, and contemplation may have been minimal.

Having time for reflection, endeavoring to overcome conflicting emotions and delusory mental states and so on, would most likely be very difficult under those circumstances. Thus the monastery was seen as a haven for such pursuits.

Focusing on the Experience, not the Object

From the Buddhist point of view, it is the experience of desire that is emphasized, not the object of our desire. We cannot superimpose the external object as being problematic as if the object is the problem rather than the personal or inner response and experience.

It is always possible that one may lose oneself and become besotted by a new love, even if the person has a questionable or unattractive character. Or it may be due to an obsession over an inanimate object, that one can become completely overwhelmed and lose oneself over. One may become desperate for that person or object and go through all kinds of inner trauma and turmoil. The cause is the samsaric mind. That is what samsara is. It is not about the external object. One could be totally obsessed with an object so insignificant, something without meaning for anybody else, but for that individual it has become the most important thing.

Buddhism tries to address these types of issues. It is not about saying the world is evil or the world is not evil. Samsara is not evil either but the samsaric experience is dissatisfactory. It is not evil; it is just dissatisfactory. It causes relentless discontentment and frustration and is the main source of our anxiety. That is why we need to be wary of it. Sometimes, even in our relationships, even on a very practical level, we may need to take some time out and see what is going on within our lives.

By becoming a monk or a nun, one is not retiring from the world but rather, taking time out to a degree so that one can engage in self-reflection and have a better understanding of oneself and the world. It is a lifestyle choice that hopefully provides some reduction in distractions, such as the responsibility of raising a family. In monastic life and retreat, one can be more in tune with what is really going on with oneself, rather than getting caught up in the delusory mental states that Buddhism speaks about, mental states such as seeing our primary problem as external. Conflicting emotions can be debilitating and destructive and when negative desires become unceasing it can disrupt and diminish our lives.

Part of the monastic's training is in how to utilize positive forms of desire; it is not to renounce desire altogether. The monk or nun is learning how to distinguish the positive desire from the negative desires that we so often become caught up in. As we have been discussing, which is true for the ordained members of the sangha as well, by developing positive forms of desire, one learns how to overcome the negative desire forms. In this way the monastic learns how to be resolute, how to aspire towards the positive. In so doing, one is not condemned by their weakness but strengthened through the generation of positive altruistic desires. One could say that the main difference between a monastic and a lay practitioner is the lifestyle.

In Buddhism, a person who is totally given over to the samsaric currents of life is seen as a very weak person, a person who gets easily blown around, tossed about in the turbulent waters of samsara. As stated in Buddhist literature, one is tossed about without any control. Whether a lay practitioner or a Buddhist monastic, the teachings and training is to become stronger through harnessing the positive forms of desire so that the individual will have the willpower to work with the negative forms of desire rather than being overwhelmed by them.

Monastic training does not just involve mindfulness and awareness and the practice of meditation. The ordained sangha member also undergoes training in how to think clearly, through study, debate, and so on. This training relates back to the idea of wrong view, right view, and no view, which was explained earlier. Throughout all Buddhist training there is an emphasis on how to overcome the negative forms of our desirous nature by utilizing the positive desire forms. In so doing the first step is focused on correcting the wrong views that one holds about oneself.

When someone follows the Dharma as a practitioner, renunciant, or monastic they are not embarking on a path to contemplate the evils of the world as such. They are there to contemplate on the self to see, "How do I experience the world and how do I respond to the world? What is my experience?" This is done through cultivation of mindfulness and awareness. It is not about what the world is like as an external entity, but about how one experiences and responds to the world.

That is where the practitioner, renunciant, and monastic should begin. Through contemplation and meditation, one can realize which of my experiences are based on grasping and clinging. All practitioners may see that whenever they have an experience of something, they latch onto it or grasp and cling onto it. We have many different kinds of experiences but, automatically, due to our preponderance towards certain habitual tendencies, we pick something out and get fixated on that. Through reasoning, one begins to develop the correct view. The wrong view is to think that objects or experiences are unique, and can exist all by itself, independently, without causes and conditions.

The point in Buddhism is that the mind has a tendency to automatically latch onto something and turn it into what it is not. Therein lies our samsaric downfall. When we have latched onto a person or an object, we superimpose our desires and expectations onto it. This arouses strong emotions and conviction in us, through our belief that our perception is the solid reality. The emotional investment and conviction in our own personal reality is very strong. Not only are there strong emotions and convictions arising in relation to what we perceive on the sensory level, but intellectually we support our developing convictions with our thoughts and stories. Because of that we get entrapped in the delusory, samsaric state. That is how the delusory samsaric experiences are perpetuated and supported. Through our emotional conviction and the use of the intellect, we develop a plausible case to support our beliefs and their subsequent responses.

Therefore, right from the beginning, all practitioners, including ordained members of the sangha, try to learn about that process. The practitioner tries to understand that about themselves, rather than focusing on the materiality of whatever the desirable object might be, be it a car, a house, or a sentient being.

From a Buddhist perspective, we are not demonizing or denigrating the objects of our experiences or emotional responses. When we look at how we apprehend the world, we are trying to understand ourselves in terms of how we respond to the world—animate and inanimate—and how that engagement gives rise to disturbance in us. That is what Buddhism is more interested in. Buddhism is interested in what leads to less disturbance in the mind and what creates more disturbance in the mind. The *source* of the disturbance is not where the focus should lie. What may give rise to disturbance in one person may not necessarily give rise to disturbance in another person. Therefore, disturbance in the mind does not ultimately have to do with the external object.

How the object is perceived still has the major significance, of course. The object in itself may not be as important but it is how the object is perceived that is important. From a Buddhist point of view, in terms of how to overcome our grasping tendencies, it is not simply to gain more insight into an understanding of how we respond to things in a very impulsive way. It is also about the perception of the object—that is, the things that we get very worked up about. It may be something that we really despise and have aversion to or something we have attraction to.

Our responses of attraction and aversion to an object are another aspect of desire with distinctive characteristics that also lead to grasping and fixation. It is important to remember that even aversion has an element of desire.

Understanding how we perceive the object is important. Not only in terms of its attractive qualities or its repulsive qualities but, in itself, intellectually, how do we seize or apprehend it? How does our cognitive process work? To put it in other words, how does our cognitive process work when we cognize something as being attractive or unattractive? When we apprehend a physical object, such as a car or house, what sort of process is going on for us? Further, how does that generate an emotional response and all the investment that we put into what we have perceived? In Buddhism all these considerations are taken into account. This will be discussed in more detail in Part 2 of this book.

We should not only try to understand it in terms of our emotions and feelings—what sorts of physical feelings we have when we become emotionally aroused or what sorts of emotions move us—but cognitively, also, we can check on how we are seizing an object.

So a Buddhist monk or nun, through the practice of *satipaṭṭhāna* meditation, using mindfulness and awareness, can begin to have some understanding of what is really going on in the mind[14]. One develops an understanding that the mind is very selective, that the mind only chooses to settle itself on certain objects and that the mind singles things out and then blows those things out of all proportion through its responsiveness. Our responses become all-consuming and can overwhelm the mind to the extent that potentially, the mind becomes oblivious to everything else.

The monastic or renunciant sangha member recognizes that this is happening not just on the emotional level but, at the deeper level, the cognitive structure of the mind can be seen to have a tendency to a more narrow focus. So they can ask themselves, "Why am I focusing all of my attention on this particular thing? Why not something else?"

Of course, in Buddhist practice, we are not talking about diffusing our attention. In Buddhism, mindfulness practice and awareness practice does entail focusing our mind so it is not getting diffused. We should not think that it does not matter if our mind is scattered instead of blinkered. It is also not appropriate to think, "I should not be so fixated on certain things" or "I should not be grasping at certain things. Therefore, then I should just let anything and everything come up and not be bothered by them." That is not the Buddhist perspective either. Buddhism emphasizes, as I mentioned, the need for mindfulness and awareness, in order to be attentive to what is going on in the mind. It is important to develop an awareness of the distinction between grasping, clinging, and fixation, and the state of being attentive.

In other words, there is a way to attend, to be attentive, without getting fixated. Getting fixated is what we do habitually. Everything else within our experience can become insignificant and recede into the background, while fixation becomes almost an assault to our senses. "I must have this or that object if I am going to experience any peace at all."

The process of choosing to pay attention is different from what happens when something grabs our attention. When we yield to whatever it is that grabs our attention, we are expressing a lack of control. That is, we have become slaves automatically to whatever sensory experience takes our attention.

In Buddhism then, we talk about how to be attentive without chasing after—without hankering after—without getting all caught up with something. The object could be the same but our relationship to it and our sensory responsiveness has changed. So, for example, whatever the monastic or renunciant experiences the most problems with, from a desire perspective, they will focus their mind on that to develop the ability to pay attention and understand what is going on. That kind of focus is the focus of all practitioners, not just monastics and is different from the monastics' other concerns, that which captures their attention in leading an appropriate monastic life—being mindful of their routines and responsibilities, as well as continuously applying mindfulness within their cloistered environments.

So from a Buddhist point of view, that is how practitioners, even ordained members of the sangha, should be working with negative kinds of desire. That is what we all need to focus on. It is not about the object so therefore it is not about the world that the object is part of. Through understanding that, one corrects the misunderstanding that this is something that arises independently of everything else as something unique. That misunderstanding is also dispensed with as part of one's meditation. Through meditation one can realize that it is not the object that is unique. The uniqueness comes from the unique way in which we choose to pay attention to that object. The object that seizes our attention is not particularly unique. The uniqueness of that object is a result of our mind choosing to see it that way, as if the object is in isolation.

So correct understanding, the right view, is about reversing that tendency and seeing that what we think is unique, so unbelievably unique, is part of a pattern, part of an interconnecting field of factors and events which will be discussed in more detail in part 2. It is important to recognize interdependence or what is referred to as dependently arising.

Chapter 7
Interdependence

Something can be unique on the relative level,[15] but it is unique only in relation to other things within that category. On the absolute level, to say something is unique—that is something different. From the Buddhist way of thinking, even when we talk about the concept of something being unique or important, and it really captures our imagination or grabs our attention, it does so in context. It does so in relation to other things: there is a reference point for something being unique in relation to other things being more common or more ordinary.

Automatically, the uniqueness of that object or individual is diminished because it loses some of its self-sufficient, unique quality when seen in context. Whatever unique quality that individual or object possesses has to be measured in relation to other things that are not as unique as that individual object, person, or experience. From the Buddhist point of view, this is seen as a very important insight.

So the practice of mindfulness and awareness is just the first step. We grasp and cling onto things because of our wrong views, as has been discussed. To correct that, we have to think with more clarity and develop an understanding of the correct view. The correct view considers that everything is interconnected, pratītyasamutpāda—dependently arisen, and that internal and external phenomena co-arise. Objects do not arise independently of each other. This view provides us with a new perspective to see our individual experience as being not so personal, and what is external as being not so public or separate from our personal experience.

What is internal, what is external, what is personal, and what is public begin to blend into each other. We choose not to recognize that normally, but in reality what we experience in ourselves and what is out there in the world is not so clear-cut. There are no demarcation lines that we can draw. We can believe that there is a boundary line where "my personal experiences cease and the public external sphere begins," but that is not the case. That is not to say that they are the same.

Dependent arising is a very important concept. It is said that if we have an understanding of that notion of phenomena "dependently arising," we will grasp and cling less onto what we experience. Therefore we will be more engaged with the full gamut of our experiences.

As the first step, we try to get used to that notion through meditation. Through developing mindfulness and awareness in meditation we become aware of how our minds grasp onto and fixate on things. That has to be followed by the practice of *vipaśyanā*, insight meditation, coupled with an understanding of pratītyasamutpāda, dependent arising, which is what vipaśyanā is about.

This has to be done even in relation to ourselves by understanding what it is we are referring to when we speak of the *self*. Self can be seen as the five *skandhas*, or five aggregates. The five aggregates are: body, feelings, volitional dispositions, our cognitive faculty, and consciousness. These five constitute what we call our "self" but what does that mean? It means there is no such thing as a self that we can fixate on as something unique, something existing by itself.

We have a notion about ourselves purely because we have a body. That body took birth at a certain time, that body grew up somewhere, in certain places, and that body happens to be the locus for our experiences insofar as feelings go. The body is obviously not inanimate, not like a table or chair—*bem po* in Tibetan. Our body is animate so therefore the body has feelings; the body can experience pain, pleasure, and so forth. We also have a mind and, like the body, it is not something that is unitary, that we can fixate on. There are different forms of consciousness or mind. There is a consciousness that we are conscious of. Just by being conscious there is consciousness, which is the seat of thinking and creating. We also have sense consciousnesses. There is consciousness of the visual organ, the nasal organ, the aural organ, the taste organ, the touch organ, and mental events. In part 2 there is further discussion of the senses.

If we think of the mind as unitary, then we have separated our mind from our body and they then become unitary aspects. This position creates a separation between body and mind, which is an example of the wrong view. The right view recognizes that the body and mind both have many different elements. For example, when we have feelings, experience our cognitive capacity, memories, and so on, all experiences and manifestations come together as mind.

When we begin to understand ourselves in that way, we have less fixation on the self as being definitively *me*. Whenever we say: "this is me," we should be asking the questions: "In what context is this me? What do I mean 'this is me'? This is me in relation to what?"

From a Buddhist point of view, we should not get too fixated on what we call "the mind" or "the body" as existing all by itself. The body is there conditionally, sustaining itself because of a variety of factors. As long as propitious circumstances continue to flourish, we will have this body intact. In the case of disease, sickness, and death, that body will disintegrate. From the Buddhist point of view then, the body is sustained because of various physical and biological factors. It needs to be a properly functioning system so life can be prolonged.

So there can be different perspectives on what we think of ourselves as a body, as a mind, and the relationship between the two. We may give the mind many different labels like "soul, psyche, inner self, higher self," or whatever the case might be. We may also relate to certain aspects of ourselves as being "the real me" and think everything else is false, or "not really me," because we become fixated on who we believe ourselves to be.

To overcome fixation, the monastics and the lay practitioners need to overcome that misunderstanding and recognize the self or the mind, the body, and the world as being interdependent. The mind is dependent on the body, the body is dependent on the mind; mind and body are dependent on the world. The world, in turn, is not so very different from the physically embodied individual because the individual is connected to the physical environment mentally, social, physically, and in other ways. Developing that perspective helps to correct the idea, the wrong view that things exist in isolation.

Chapter 8
Where Samsara Resides

In Buddhism, even the concept of desire is not something that we should fixate on. There is no such thing as desire *per se*, to be taken as some kind of unitary concept or entity because there are so many different kinds of desire. Some, dependent on the context, should be cultivated, and others we should learn to overcome, or transcend as we have been discussing.

We may think of desire in a very black and white way, that is, we can either abandon desire altogether, or have a very positive attitude towards it as if there is no real problem with it—both approaches are wrong insofar as these are forms of fixation. It would be completely in tune with Buddhism then if we did not fixate on the concept of desire as something to be either cultivated or rejected but, rather, tried to understand the nature and complexity of desire so that we can correct some of the misconceptions and misunderstandings about it.

In Buddhism, the notion of renunciation is emphasized, which stems from the early Buddhist point of view. When renunciation is seen as such an essential part of Buddhist practice, we have to exercise some caution not to misunderstand what is being worked with and renounced. We should not jump to the conclusion that when Buddhists speak about renunciation, when we speak about the worthiness of leading a celibate life or becoming a monastic and leading a renunciant life, it is not done to turn away from the world. It is not done to turn away from the world in such a way that the object of desire is either demonized or seen as something bad.

In Buddhism, we do not think of the world and sensory objects as the Devil's playground and we do not speak about temptation and things of that kind, as is done in some religious contexts. For example, there is no myth of the *fall into temptation* in Buddhism. So there is no real concept of temptation in that regard, nor the undesirable consequences that follow from an original experience of temptation. Therefore, in Buddhism, as discussed, when renunciation and celibacy are emphasized, it has more of a practical point to it, rather than one based on a metaphysical or mythological narrative. We are not seen as evil, nor is the world itself seen to be evil.

In Buddhism, the problem is not seen to be with the world; the problem lies in our response to the world and our relationship with our experiences. Therefore, practitioners, be they laity or monastic, train in how to understand themselves better so that they will not respond to the world in a negative way and continue to experience the misery of samsara. Samsara is seen as existing in the mind; samsara is not the world taken as a whole. Samsara is in the mind of the individual because of our sensory experiences, deep-seated habits, strong emotions, and the delusory mental states that we are immersed in. As a result, from the moment of our birth, it is very difficult for us to engage with the world properly and fully.

We are adrift when we are confused in samsara. When we are tossed about by strong currents of emotion, we grasp onto certain experiences as real, to help provide certainty. It is said that being in samsara is like being carried away by the strong current of a river. Samsara is compared to a river. The turbulence within our minds is compared to the turbulence of the water. Our efforts to grasp onto various sensory objects, ideas, beliefs, abstract concepts, and experiences, are like clutching onto pieces of wood being carried down the river. We try in desperation to clutch onto the wood, in order to find some kind of secure ground.

Thus a renunciant or a lay practitioner may take time out and devote themselves to understanding the mind. One does this by training the mind by using mindfulness and other meditational practices, to try to gain insight into how the mind works. With the exercise of mindfulness and awareness, the mind can slow down and we can more easily observe the mind's activities. Unless the mind's frantic pace, the frenzy of mental activity, slows down somewhat, we cannot even have a glimpse of how the mind is working. If we do not understand how the mind works, we cannot overcome grasping and clinging and it will be relentless, because our mind will remain totally outward-directed.

With the practice of mindfulness and awareness we learn to see how our mind is grasping onto all kinds of things. The practice of mindfulness and awareness is seen in itself as a way of learning how to reduce our tendency to grasp and cling. It is harder to refrain from grasping when we see something—the visual sense, or hear something—the aural sense. Right from the beginning with the practice of meditation, one tries to learn not to react to one's thoughts, emotions, and feelings, as they arise during meditation. That is how we begin to observe the mind's activities. This process whereby we let go of being highly reactive, within itself helps us to recognize our grasping nature, and we then learn how to grasp less onto activity in the mind.

As we relax the tendency to grasp onto our mental activity within meditation, we find this filters through to our post-meditation. The next time we see something that would normally overwhelm or overpower us, we can find that the intensity of our fixated response has lessened. Thus the mind is less disturbed.

Our mind is so selective. It only chooses to fix onto those things that we ourselves find desirable or of interest. These are singled out from a whole range of sensory phenomena that are all interconnected. Therefore, as soon as we make that selection, we lose the wider vision. We lose proper perspective because we become mono-focal or myopic. It is similar to putting blinkers on: we cannot see left or right and the peripheral is ignored. When that happens, our vision—what we think we are experiencing, becomes totally distorted. Similarly, from this point of view, the mono-focal view operates like that with our delusory mental states, where we grasp onto a thought or emotion, and react to it out of all proportion to the context.

The practice of mindfulness and awareness requires us to exercise attentiveness. There is a big difference between the mono-focus of the grasping samsaric mind and the mind that is open, relaxed, mindful, attentive, and aware. The samsaric mind is totally focused on something, but with total confusion, agitation, excitement, and little or no awareness.

When we apply attentiveness in meditation, we are paying attention to and focusing on an object, such as the breath or a statue. As we do that, it is with a sense of awareness so that we are not thrown into a state of agitation or confusion. Therefore, when we focus our mind on the object of meditation, we do not lose sight of the panorama within the mind. We remain in touch with the horizon or the background of the object of our mental focus, but in a non-grasping way. In Buddhism, through the practice of mindfulness, we learn how to focus without fixation and without grasping onto whatever it is we are focusing on.

When we are thrown into a deep state of confusion, we become mono-focal, one-pointed in a distorted way, without any notion of foreground or background experience or of a field of experience, because we are simply too obsessed with the object of desire itself. We really need to understand that when we exercise mindfulness and focus our mind in meditation, it is totally different from the obsessive, compulsive way we focus on something we are completely consumed with. In the latter case, when the mind obsessively returns again and again to the same place in a mono-focal way, that is a different kind of mental focus.

Learning to focus and pay attention more effectively can begin to liberate us from grasping, clinging, and fixation. When we practice mindfulness and awareness with our mental states, we are gradually learning not to grasp or cling. For example, when a strong emotion arises, rather than homing in on the emotion and being shaken, disturbed, or distracted by it, we can remain as an observer, allowing the emotion to subside in its own time.

Initially, when we begin this practice, we can try a form of self-talk, engaging in a type of monologue to assist us: "Well, just let it pass, don't dwell on it, don't get too worked up or take it too seriously." This way, the next time a strong emotion or disturbing thought arises it is less likely we will be perturbed by it. We will be less fixated and will not grasp onto that thought or emotion.

In Buddhism, the monastic sangha and the laity alike, as practitioners, need to learn to maintain awareness so that when they encounter a visual or aural stimulus, they are able to maintain a sense of mental equilibrium, even if they have seen or heard something wonderful, unexpected, or amazing[16].

Two methods of meditation: Śamatha *or Tranquility Meditation and* Vipaśyanā *or Analytical Meditation*

With both techniques—śamatha and vipaśyanā, one is learning to cultivate mindfulness and awareness. With vipaśyanā one learns to see dependent arising, rather than experiencing the world as being made up of independent entities. In meditation, when we have certain thoughts and emotions arising, we do not need to latch onto such mental activity. We do not immediately fix onto what arises but rather, we see the thought or emotion arising in a certain context—that is, as a product of particular causes and conditions. What arises becomes part of our mental fabric or the fabric of our experience of the world. It does not need to be rejected. In meditation, emotions and mental events should be given room to arise and dissipate without excessive engagement.

Our tendency to single out a particular thought or emotion in meditation and fixate on it, judge it, and be distracted by it, is an example of our tendency to see things in isolation rather than as interconnected. If we find the thoughts and emotions pleasant and develop attraction, or if we find them unpleasant and develop aversion, this process may disturb our equilibrium and create a distorted view within meditation. And it can be argued that when fully engrossed in critically judging our thoughts, we are not applying mindfulness. Rather, we are following our normal samsaric habit-patterns and disturbing our own mind.

In meditation we can encounter and recognize what is going on in the mind in a less grasping and fixated way instead of singling out a particular thought and focusing our mind on that—"this is jealousy" or "this is joy" or "this is anger." From the perspective of vipaśyanā, we can observe the activity in the mind in relation to the different forms the mind can take, trying to see an interconnected panorama of experience, inclusive of the different forms of the mind.

As with the mind, the body is not seen as something inert, something totally material. It is seen as being in a state of motion, constantly changing, in constant flux, like the mind. There is movement in both body and mind and the movement is interconnected. We can be aware and observe the display of the body and mind in an inclusive and enriched way within our meditation without it being a distraction and without having to narrow down our focus. Applying mindfulness and awareness in meditation does not involve shutting out or shutting down anything to do with our experience and this includes our immediate external environment and the interchange and interconnectedness of ourselves and the world. It is about being the observer of the movement and flux of the mind and body, while remaining open and aware and relaxing our tendency to grasp and fixate.

We do this to see more clearly how the mind works and to help us recognize the relationship between our mind and the world. To help the analysis process in vipaśyanā meditation, we can investigate and ask ourselves where that movement comes from. In essence, the movement in the body-mind complex, that state of motion of both body and mind, comes from us being connected to things other than our own physicality and mental world, because of the interconnectedness of all things, pratītyasamutpāda, dependent arising. So understanding pratītyasamutpāda is the antidote to wrong view, which is negative, because it is the right view, which is inclusive and positive. As previously mentioned, we have to have right view to correct the wrong view; and then we can go beyond all views.

Thus, one learns the practice of vipaśyanā meditation to correct the wrong view. So with vipaśyanā meditation, the practitioner or monastic learns to go beyond the process of grasping onto a particular thought or emotion, and to understand that everything that we experience is a product of many factors. Whatever it is that one is thinking, one automatically sees its interconnection rather than seeing it as something existing by itself, in itself.

Whatever we might be thinking about, whether it is to do with the mental world or the external, physical world—particularly with the physical world, we can choose to see physical phenomena as not solid, nor existing all by themselves. Instead of focusing on the thing-hood or thing-ness[17] of a particular object, one can think about the "horizon" of that object. Whatever we are focusing our mind on, the object in question, is more broadly connected to or hooked up with many other things.

This seemingly unique and individually present object which we experience through our senses is, in fact, something that we have chosen to focus our mind on. That object, whether it is a table or chair, is present to us in relationship with many other things. They are also equally present to our senses. Realizing that, then we can see the arising and cessation of entities. This is how it is expressed in early Buddhism—"the arising and cessation of entities and objects." Instead of focusing on the thing-ness or thing-hood of various physical objects that we encounter, we can develop understanding of how they arise, sustain, then cease.

Using the example of the chest of drawers again, we are attracted to it and we focus our mind on the piece of furniture. We think it looks beautiful in the furniture shop window and we develop a strong desire to have this piece. In that way, we isolate the chest of drawers and it becomes the object of our main focus. We can make use of our responses in this context to look at how we apprehend things and how we see the world generally. Then we can contemplate less myopically on how our desire for such an object was created and how our tendency to grasp onto it and other objects could be reduced. We see that the chest of drawers is a product, that it has come into being from a carefully selected tree with the appropriate wood for such a piece of furniture. The tree is cut and the wood is fashioned in a series of steps to produce the chest of drawers that we love. We can consider the human beings and the varying skills they have developed to both collect and transport the wood, the carpentry and cabinet-making skills, and the factory and machinery used to make the furniture. We can then come to see how so many disparate elements are involved in producing this particular chest of drawers.

From the Buddhist point of view, trying to understand things in this way is not just a vain intellectual exercise. If we begin to think about many other things in this way as well, it will give us insight into a more inclusive understanding of and a connection to how things arise and dissipate. If we have a more acute awareness of how things come into being and how they cease to be, and recognize their interdependence, our tendency to grasp and cling onto things so myopically will diminish and a broader, more inclusive perspective will eventually predominate.

When we are in a state of delusion, we are convinced our normal way of thinking really reflects the way the world is, and we may think that to have a spiritual or alternative perspective on what we experience may make us ungrounded, other-worldly, or may force us to turn our attention away from the world. From the Buddhist perspective, a more inclusive view of how things come into being—arise and dissipate—really allows us to see the world in its proper perspective.

Therefore, in many respects, it is the practitioner, the renunciant who really becomes the worldly person. By developing an understanding of the arising and cessation of things in the world and how the world actually functions, one becomes more truly connected to the world. There is nothing wrong with the arising and cessation of things. From the point of view of early Buddhism, if we have that understanding, we will have less grasping and clinging onto things, less fixation, and we will be more in tune with the world. Therefore, we will be happier.

In terms of our internal, mental world, and the external, physical world there will then be some kind of correspondence, a more harmonious relationship, between the two. A monastic, lay practitioner, or renunciant comes to understand that, both in the internal world of the mental experience, and the external world of sensory experience, nothing remains the same. As we recognize that nothing remains the same, we find it more difficult to fixate on a given form, say, as we know that that form will change.

As far as Buddhism is concerned, we are driven by the need for security, by the need to find some kind of secure ground. That is why we get obsessed and desperate, wanting to latch onto objects, emotions, thoughts, and ideas. There is a lot of variety in the things we crave, the things we believe will give us security. We can be desperately in need of love, wealth, power, influence, and many other things. These may deliver some security on the relative level, but in time, this too will change.

Although one may have come to the understanding that everything is in a state of flux or is transient, nevertheless Buddhism does emphasize the importance of stability. That is the interesting thing about what Buddha instructed his disciples to do. The Buddha emphasized the importance of developing stability in the face of flux, and without fixation. That is truly the main insight that Buddha continued to return to in his teachings: that through the practice of meditation, we can learn to find stability.

Stability has nothing to do with fixation. We can have stability in the face of a myriad experiences and changes going on in our lives. The changing, unsettled nature of the world cannot be changed. That is how the world is and we have no power over that. In the face of such uncertainty, instead of desperately creating a facsimile of a fixed reality and latching onto that for dear life, we can learn to have a sense of stability within us. This is best developed through the practice of meditation, and through a greater understanding of the world. Within the turbulence, there can be stability. That is the key to non-grasping.

Non-grasping produces a sense of stability that defuses desperation. There is no impetus for us to become frantic and frenzied. In that way, we can develop a fundamental sense of equilibrium within, despite all the goings-on of life, both internally and externally.

It is not just the world that is in a state of flux but it also happens within ourselves, in terms of what we call the "five psychophysical constituents."[18] We see ourselves changing, we see it physically, mentally, in relation to our feelings, in relation to our volitional dispositions, in terms of how we process various kinds of information about the world, and how we perceive things. In relation to the five psychophysical constituents, we can also see continuous change.

Through developing the right view of dependent arising and practicing mindfulness and awareness, we will have stability, despite the changes we perceive. Through developing this kind of stability, we are in a better position to progress. Despite the flurried activity that goes on externally and internally, there will be some degree of stable development in how we evolve and develop as individuals, especially when we have embarked on the path of the Dharma.

In summary, the first way to overcome grasping is to practice mindfulness and awareness. The second way is to correct the wrong view with the right view, which comes from understanding how the world is and from the understanding of the five psychophysical constituents, while seeing the interconnected nature of all things.

We have spoken about going beyond understanding, *going beyond view*. "Going beyond view" means going beyond understanding. We have to do more than simply *understand* the arising and cessation of things; we actually have to come to experience this ourselves, practically speaking. If that happens, we will have gone beyond simple understanding and beyond even a profound understanding of how things arise and cease. Going beyond understanding is the ultimate form of going beyond fixation—we have let go of the last form of fixation.

First, we suffer from this malignancy of grasping onto things. We latch on onto them while misunderstanding the nature and interconnectedness of that which we are grasping onto. Thus we suffer, as a consequence of our lack of understanding. So we try to correct that through the practice of śamatha meditation, exercising willpower or conviction, and vipaśyanā, or insight meditation, to gain more understanding.

We must develop understanding, and recognize that everything arises and ceases. Even more than understanding, we have to have a deep realization that that is how the world is. With such a deep realization, we do not need to think about the changing, interconnected nature of all things because we simply embody that as our experience. So the ultimate aim is to go beyond even the understanding that corrects all the misunderstandings we have accumulated over a long period of time.

To convert understanding into direct insight we need to make a distinction between understanding and insight or realization. The difference between them is that understanding is conceptual, even though it can also contain some insight; whereas true insight is non-conceptual, as is realization. When one directly experiences the true nature of things it can be described as "embodying the teachings," as if one is breathing life into the theory.

In Buddhism the three practices are emphasized. We find this even in early Buddhism. Some have said the idea of *going beyond all views* is a Mahayana concept and that early Buddhism did not contain this idea, and they believe that it was a Mahayana import into Buddhism. However, that is not the case. In early Buddhism, in some suttas the Buddha did speak about going beyond all views. Further, the Buddha spoke about going beyond all forms of understanding. So what is meant by that is that going beyond fixation can only be completely and totally achieved when we go beyond an intellectual understanding about ourselves.

That is the framework within which Buddhist practitioners should try to work with grasping, clinging, and fixation. The same idea carries through into Mahayana Buddhism and Tantricism. In Mahayana Buddhism, mindfulness and awareness are seen as essential. They give us the key and the starting point we need, to slow our mind down.

The frenzied environment within which the mind works is responsible for all the agitation that we experience. When the mind becomes clearer and less frenetic we can see how it is responding to itself, the sensory input, and the world. With that improved insight we can respond to our emotions, thoughts, and feelings in a less agitated way. We can give room for our experiences to arise and fall without allowing ourselves to be too bothered by them. This approach promotes calmness in the face of internal and external turmoil. Calming the mind provides us with the space and perspective to look at mind's activity and responsiveness, thus bringing into being more understanding and insight into the reactive and obsessive tendencies of the mind.

We are dependent on that calmness to develop understanding. In Mahayana, the understanding that we try to develop is not so very different from that advanced in early Buddhism. The notion in early Buddhism of *arising and cessation* is referred to as *emptiness* in Mahayana Buddhism. It is often also referred to as *insubstantiality*. From the Mahayana perspective, if we really want to let go of grasping, clinging, and fixation, we have to develop some understanding of emptiness or insubstantiality. The notion of emptiness keeps us from attaching too much significance to our response to what we encounter on a daily basis.

Understanding emptiness will free us from that tendency to concretize and solidify everything. Contemplating the empty or insubstantial nature of all things challenges our tendency to see it all as quite rigid, inflexible, inert, and fixed. The notion of emptiness is built on the understanding of everything as arising and ceasing. As Buddha himself said, his most important gift to his disciples was the understanding of pratītyasamutpāda, dependent arising—how things arise and cease.

Nagarjuna[19] and other prominent Mahayana masters also elaborated on the concept of emptiness which is based on the notion of dependent arising. Our tendency to see the world differently from how it actually exists means we get fixated on the thing-ness of things, like the table-ness of the table or the chair-ness of the chair or the mountain-ness of the mountain. By fixating the mind on the table-ness or chair-ness, we see that as something very definite, as if the concept itself is solid and real, existing by itself, as it were, and that is the wrong conception.

When we relate the concept of emptiness to objects, it means they are empty of table-ness, chair-ness, mountain-ness, and the like. In other words, even though we have these terms and labels and we use definitions, there are no real, fixed referents to any of these objects. Whatever referent there may be is only conventionally constructed, as part of our linguistic practice and usage. In reality there is nothing that has substance outside of what is constructed by our minds.

The concept of table-ness and chair-ness has more to do with how we use our concepts and the conventional usage of our linguistic practices, rather than how things actually exist. Therefore, from a Mahayana point of view, there is no fixed table-ness or chair-ness that we can hang onto. We assign qualities and characteristics to objects and experiences but an object or experience does not itself possess these qualities or attributes. These are all mental imputations.

Realizing that does not only give us intellectual understanding of how things are or how things work. In fact, recognizing how much influence and impact our conceptual activity—attraction, aversion; like, dislike, and so on—has on what we experience, has a transformative effect on us. We need not grasp at things so tenaciously. So when we see a table or chair or some other object, any strong emotions and feelings that may arise associated with that object and created by our mind, may not be as forceful or as frequent.

Chapter 9
Correcting our Misapprehension of the World

In Mahayana, the point of the practice of vipaśyanā, analytical or insight meditation, and of meditation on emptiness, is to correct the misunderstanding that there is something apart from our conceptual linguistic conventions that exists in a real way pertaining to objects such as tables and chairs and so on.

Of course, we have to use concepts and we have to rely on our conventional practice of linguistic usage and so forth. From a Mahayana perspective, it is important to understand those mechanics. We can continue to use those same concepts, and to use the language in the same way, while simultaneously understanding that this is no more than a conventional practice. There is no absolute correspondence between how things actually are and how we use our concepts and language. Although there is a relationship, language does not necessarily mirror the reality that we are trying to apprehend. Language is not necessarily a veil that obscures, but it does not transparently represent reality. This is the gist of the Mahayanist view.

Thus we can see linguistic usage as a relative and conventional practice. We do not need to see language as describing reality perfectly, in an absolute sense. It does not represent reality on an absolute level but, rather, it is helpful on a practical level for daily situations.

Understanding things in that way also helps us overcome grasping and clinging, and that understanding comes from meditation on emptiness or insubstantiality. So to think of meditation on emptiness as too philosophical, intellectual, or abstract is incorrect. Understanding insubstantiality or emptiness is directly related and can bring benefit to our ordinary, everyday life.

Throughout the centuries, female and male Buddhist masters of all schools have emphasized the importance of vipaśyanā meditation. Not only should we cultivate mindfulness and awareness, but we should also try to develop understanding about the world and ourselves by paying more attention to the world and to ourselves. If we engage with that, we can see it is true: we can recognize the insubstantial quality and experience emptiness directly. It is not an understanding or experience that we have to wait until enlightenment or the next life for.

Deepening the understanding of śūnyatā or emptiness can also have the effect of eroding our tendency to grasp, cling, and be fixated on things. This allows us to engage with our sensory experiences in a much freer and more liberated and liberating way. We have developed a sense of openness to sensory experiences so that we have a broader and more inclusive experience.

Mahayana also says that when there is less grasping and clinging, our sensory experiences become cleansed and purified. In fact, far from discouraging us from enjoying our sensory experiences, Buddhism maintains that we will enjoy them more if we do not get too attached—clinging, grasping, and craving for things. If one is not feeling so frantic and desperate, then what we experience will be experienced more fully and more completely.

The concept of emptiness is not something that we have to understand at the expense of our attention to sensory objects, the phenomenal appearance of tables, chairs, and so forth. The emptiness is embodied in the object, be it a table, chair, or anything else.

If we are not so desperate and frantic and there is a sense of openness and lightness of being, we will see emptiness or insubstantiality in the objects. That is the point—the appearance of reality, the coalescing of appearance and reality—reality is not hidden by appearance. Reality is hidden from us only because of our delusory mental states. If our delusions are reduced through greater awareness, through the greater practice of mindfulness and greater understanding, we will continue to have the experience of appearance, but appearance will be perceived as not being separate from reality, reality being emptiness—that is, appearance and emptiness together.

As the Heart Sutra has said, "Form is nothing other than emptiness; emptiness is nothing other than form." From a Mahayana perspective, that is the key to understanding how we should think about the relationship between phenomenal appearance and reality. There is nothing wrong with how things appear to us. Our concern with appearance is that when our minds are myopic and confused, and they grasp onto an aspect of the appearance, we distort reality. When there is less tendency to grasp or be obsessed, we can perceive appearance in a more genuine and panoramic way. By seeing the interconnected and insubstantial nature of appearance we will see that appearance and reality are not separate.

We can also express that by saying that ultimate truth and relative truth are not separate. Relative truth is the form that the ultimate truth assumes. Ultimate truth, in itself, does not have any form so therefore it cannot be perceived either with our mind's eye or with our physical organs. If ultimate truth is perceived at all, it is perceived through appearance. The relative and absolute truths are non-separable.

When we grasp and cling, we do not perceive ultimate truth. We even perceive relative truth in a distorted way. When our perception becomes cleansed through less grasping, clinging, and fixation, then we perceive appearance just as it appears, without distortion, and it can be seen as not being separate from emptiness.

By practicing meditation on emptiness, we correct the wrong view—the notion that physical objects have some kind of enduring essence and autonomous existence, which can be seen as a failure to understand dependent arising. In the same vein as early Buddhism, Nagarjuna said that, "Emptiness is dependent arising and dependent arising is also emptiness."

Sometimes an artificial separation has been postulated between early Buddhism and the later Mahayanists. If we read Nagarjuna, he quotes many early Buddhist sutras that are still important to the Theravadin schools of Burma, Sri Lanka, Thailand, and so on. Others have made the same point that there is a lot more commonality between Mahayana thought and early Buddhism than many people have realized.

The one additional thing that one has to do is to go beyond even that understanding, the understanding of the non-separability of relative truth and absolute truth. Through meditation, eventually one realizes the non-separability of appearance and reality, and that emptiness and phenomenal appearance are not separable. Reality is not something lofty, inaccessible, transcendental, far removed from our everyday experiences; nor is appearance completely false, deceptive, something to be dispensed with as we progress on the path. It is not the case that the appearances that used to manifest to our consciousness will cease to appear when we experience ultimate reality and that only reality will be standing there in front of us. That is not the Mahayana view. The realization of the non-separability of appearance and reality goes beyond all views, which rules out even fixation on emptiness.

The wrong way of perceiving appearance is to perceive it not as appearance but as reality—and not only as reality but, without realizing it, the samsaric mind perceives appearance in a distorted form. When contemplating emptiness and reality, we can easily become fixated on emptiness. We can make emptiness into another entity that we fixate on. Nagarjuna has warned that, in relation to phenomenal appearance, that can become a significant problem for somebody learning to go beyond grasping and clinging. Such a person may develop a kind of intellectual fixation on the notion of emptiness. They may think that everything has the nature of emptiness or that everything is emptiness, to the point of becoming nihilistic and seeing the world and everything in it as having no reality, no real significance or substance.

According to Nagarjuna, when we grasp onto the concept of emptiness incorrectly, "It is like grasping a snake wrongly. If one does not know the technique and gets hold of a snake in the wrong way, one gets bitten and then one can die."

Then Nagarjuna further cautions, saying, "If we do not understand emptiness properly, it is even more dangerous than believing appearances to be reality." So not clinging onto the concept of emptiness is the path to go beyond all views. That is seen as the final stage of going beyond fixation: to not even fixate on reality as something, to not even fixate on emptiness, to not even fixate on nirvana or the concept of Buddhahood and so on.

As we have been discussing, in order to overcome the fixation on negative mental states, negative forms of thoughts and emotions, we need to think about positive states and forms. Then we have to go beyond that. That is the way that going beyond all views, going beyond understanding, is emphasized in Mahayana Buddhism. Even if one has a profound understanding of reality, one should continue to move further and actually try to realize that reality.

To realize reality is to embody that reality. To develop understanding, one needs to accumulate knowledge; of the object of that knowledge and the subject. Buddhism speaks about degrees of knowledge, how subtle or gross the understanding is. If one has a very rough or gross understanding of reality, then there is a large gap between the subject who has the knowledge or the understanding, and the object of knowledge. The more subtle forms of understanding bridge that gap, but not completely. A very subtle distinction will remain between the object of knowledge and the subject: what is to be apprehended and the apprehender.

When one has real understanding or total realization, one goes beyond understanding in that sense, because the object of knowledge becomes embodied in the subject. Normally, when we talk about knowledge there is something to be known and the knower is the subject. But when true realization is attained, the object known does not remain something separate, even on a very subtle level. What is to be known and the knower become merged without a cognitive break between the object known and the knower, the subject.

That same idea is carried through in relation to Tantricism and even in traditions such as Mahamudra and Dzogchen[20]. Fundamentally, all the Buddhist traditions are working on the same thing: different forms of desire. Although they may often be using the methods or techniques in different ways, the point is the same. For example, in Tantricism, there is emphasis on the practice of mindfulness and awareness, on understanding reality, on recognizing how phenomena arise and cease, and on understanding the notion of emptiness. It is said in Tantra that we do not need to renounce desire but even so, negative desires still need to be transformed. There is no technique in Tantricism that says it is okay to perpetuate negative forms of desire. Tantricism says that we need to transform negative forms of desire and it uses many techniques to achieve that end.

In Tantricism, we are practicing mindfulness and awareness when we visualize a deity. We use visualization as an opportunity to stabilize and slow down the mind. So instead of focusing on the breath or an object, as we do in śamatha meditation, in Tantra, we visualize a deity. In Tantra, we keep the mind engaged by first visualizing the seed syllable of the deity, then we give rise to a sun and moon disk, and then the deity arises. We incorporate mindfulness and awareness so the flurry of mental activity begins to slow down, since we can think about only one thing at a time as we build the visualization.

The visualization helps us to experience aspects of the arising and cessation of phenomena as the deity is visually constructed and then deconstructed. At the beginning of a practice session we construct the deity out of the seed syllable or a similar symbol, and then the deity's mandala is created, which is the *arising* aspect. At the end we dissolve the visualization of the deity and of their mandala. That dissolving or dissolution of the mandala symbolizes *cessation*. The arising of the deity, and the dissipation or disappearance of the deity mimics the repeated arising and dissipating of phenomena.

Practicing Tantra and becoming familiar with the process of arising and cessation, while meditating on the notions of impermanence, insubstantiality, and emptiness, helps these concepts become more present in our minds during our daily life experience. Deity yoga serves those two purposes: the first is engaging the mind so that we learn to slow it down and practice mindfulness and awareness; and secondly, we gain insight into the continual arising and dissipating of all phenomena.

In Tantric practice, once we have dissolved the deity, we just sit quietly without entertaining thoughts, and try to rest the mind in its natural uncontrived state. *Resting in the natural state* corresponds to the experience of going beyond understanding and beyond all views. We simply remain in the natural state, unaffected by thoughts—not thinking about emptiness, not thinking about deities, not thinking about anything, just remaining in that state. Whenever we do tantric practice, we do those three things: first, we stabilize the mind; second, we develop insight into the appearance of the deity as arising and ceasing; and third, at the end of the practice session, we remain in a natural state without entertaining thought. In Mahamudra and Dzogchen teachings also, similar methods are used.

In that way then, we use those three basic stages within the method: stabilizing the mind; trying to correct the wrong view with the right view; and then going beyond all views, gaining the transcendental perspective. With each stage we learn to let go of our grasping nature. In that way we can go beyond grasping, clinging, and fixation.

As previously mentioned, fixation is more difficult to overcome. Fixation has an intellectual component to it and therefore it is important to develop correct understanding to develop the right or correct view. If we do not have the correct view, such as emptiness, or pratītyasamutpāda, which is dependent arising, we cannot overcome fixation.

We can also change our focus and analyze the *self*. If we think of the self, we are referring to something called *me*. If we pay attention, we realize that "me" is not unitary. "Me" includes my body, my feelings, my moods, my aspirations, my dreams, my memory, my sensory perceptions and faculties, and my consciousness. We can then recognize the "me" complex as changing and indefinite. Understanding that helps reduce our fixation on this notion of the self as existing all by itself in a unitary way, and this same realization can be achieved in relation to external phenomena.

Correcting these misunderstandings is very much part of Buddhist practice. Over time, we need to go beyond these misunderstandings in order to go beyond fixation. We should not remain satisfied with merely understanding the right view. If that view is very profound, such as the view of Dzogchen or Mahamudra, which is said to be a very advanced view—even so, that view should eventually give way to direct understanding and direct realization.

Many people try to make the intellectual jump from wrong view to no view, declaring that all views are bad. So, even the so-called correct view comes to be mistakenly seen as the wrong view, insofar as it is a view. Having thus decided we should not be attached to any view, we may then proclaim that we will have no views. That is not the Buddhist approach. The Buddhist way is, over time, to try to correct wrong view with right view. When one has developed a genuine understanding of sammādiṭṭhi or right view, then and only then would one have developed the capacity to leap into the state of the transcendental, the transcendence, an attainment to be equated with a high level of the enlightened state.

This concludes the general overview of desire and the pervasive samsaric tendency to grasp, cling, and fixate. Many desires may not be negative in themselves, but have become negative due to our grasping nature. We may have a certain desire which in itself, may not be a bad thing. Due to a strong negative association, however, the attending negativity can become glued to the original desire, thus causing the desire to become corrupted.

As we learn to overcome grasping and fixation, we are learning to purify desire, and by purifying desire, we learn to lead a more fulfilling life whereby we feel more at ease with the world, ourselves, and with others. We do not turn away from the world— phenomena, human intercourse and interaction—in some misguided way, as if connecting with the world has the potential to arouse different forms of desire.

As Buddhists, we try to train in how we manage desire so that even when we have desire, we manage it in a way that does not cause disruption, anxiety, or other troublesome states of mind. That seems to be the genuine aim of Buddhist practice. The aim is not to have no desire at all or to avoid desire, but to learn to overcome the negative forms of desire that are closely allied with our grasping nature and our tendency to fixate on a variety of things.

If we practice in that way, we have an understanding that does not play down the potential destructive nature of desire. We are not saying there is nothing wrong with desire. Many forms of desire are very dangerous and unproductive and extremely destructive, so we need to manage and overcome them—but having said that, we should not then take the next step and see all forms of desire as being bad.

So if we overcome the negative forms of desire that intermingle with other negative tendencies, that aids us in evolving as human beings, rather than it holding us back.

Even if one becomes fully enlightened, becomes a Buddha, does the Buddha have desire? It is a legitimate question. Of course, normally we might say, *No*. If we say the Buddha does not have desire because everything that Buddha does is out of *compassion*, then we have the question, is compassion a form of desire? It is not just a play on words if we say compassion is also a form of desire, but that type of desire is not the same as the kinds of desire that we have. Given the diverse nature of desire and the many different kinds of desire, even the Buddha perhaps could be said to have desire.

There are many different words for desire—in English what we mean by desire can encompass what in Buddhism, particularly Mahayana Buddhism, is called Buddha-intentionality[21]—so what we call "Buddha-intentionality" can be understood as a form of desire. As long as we understand that there are many different kinds of desire—and we are not saying that Buddha has the same kinds of desire as an ordinary person—there may not be any harm in saying Buddha also has desire, but it is desire of a different kind to what we have.

Even if someone has attained the transcendental state of no view and has gone beyond grasping and fixation, that enlightened individual may still have desire insofar as they have Buddha-intentionality. Buddha-intentionality should be understood as an expression of desire.

PART TWO

Abhidharma—
The Psychology of Meditation

Chapter 10
Many Elements Combine to Create Experience

The intensity of our grasping and fixation relates to the management of desire first and foremost, but also to the management of the gamut of our emotional experiences and intellectual complexities. The Buddhist tradition of meditation is practiced in order to deal with our mind and what arises in it. "How should we understand and deal with what arises in the mind?" "How is meditation practice supposed to work to overcome negative emotions or negative states of mind?" In Part 2 we will explore more broadly how human experience is created, and how we can reduce or overcome negative habit-patterns, in particular within meditational practices and contemplations.

We may think of meditation practice as a way to cultivate mindfulness, awareness, and greater concentration, and if we do that, we will automatically overcome negative states of mind. This is only partly true. We may believe doing these meditational practices will diminish the power of the negative emotions and that they will have less hold over us until they eventually disappear. While that is emphasized in Buddhist practice, it is done in a context of having gained some understanding of the mind and how it works—that is, the understanding of the psychology of meditation presented in the *Abhidharma* literature[22]. The Abhidharma, according to scholars, is based on the *sutric* and *vinaya* teachings, particularly sutra. The Abhidharma teachings are systematized and we can utilize them in order to develop a greater understanding of the mind: how it works to apprehend and make sense of the world, and how it can be transformed.

In other words, we have to put the practices of mindfulness and awareness in this context. In the Abhidharma system, mindfulness and awareness are seen as being quite different so are not treated in the same way. We may want to overcome negative states of mind and emotions and develop more positive states. In Abhidharma, then, different methods are presented for supporting the growth of positive emotions and states of mind. Additionally, Abhidharma teachings address the types of mental processes that will not produce positivity. So there is an emphasis on generating positive states, rather than the unenviable and arguably impossible task of trying to directly stamp out negativity.

As for the distinction between mindfulness and awareness, mindfulness is not only seen as being a support to positive emotions or states of mind. Mindfulness is also developed as a way of becoming more conscious of the activities in the mind in relation the range of interconnected mental events set out in the Abhidharma text. So we set out to deliberately cultivate mindfulness in terms of the variety of elements and events arising in the mind. Awareness, on the other hand, is seen as arising spontaneously as a result of successfully applying mindfulness in this way and over time, as a means of understanding the mind. As our understanding of the mind matures through the application of mindfulness, a spontaneous ability to observe the mind arises, which, as stated, is referred to as "awareness." It is not deliberately generated in the way mindfulness is. Awareness is described as one of the essential ingredients for the development of positivity. Using mindfulness and awareness to cultivate ourselves through the practice of meditation will be discussed in more detail later in part 2.

Abhidharma teachings say it is imperative that through the practice of meditation, we learn to understand the conscious mind's various "elements." The reason for this, according to Abhidharma thinking, is that as human beings we have a tendency to lump everything together into a single unit. We may believe there is something called "mind" or "consciousness," which we see as a single entity rather than a collection of functions culminating in an experience.

As Abhidharma literature explains, our conscious life is supported by varieties of mental elements, each having a different function, and therefore they speak about the "primary" and "secondary" minds. When we come to the description of emotions, reference is made to "primary positive emotions," "primary and secondary negative emotions," and varying states of mind. The idea is that if we start to understand this, we are developing knowledge about how we function and how we experience. When we investigate the mind by practicing mindfulness and awareness in meditation, we are able to use that new-found knowledge of how the mind works to detect what types of mental events are arising, and which other processes are taking place in our mind. If we did not have that background knowledge about the mind's activity and how it arises, we could forever observe thoughts coming and going and emotions arising and falling, but not gain the greater understanding to reduce our suffering and to progress on the path.

It would be just as if we were carefully watching a plant grow, shrivel up, and die. We could drop some seeds, which may begin to germinate, and then another plant may grow, and so on, but that would not help us understand anything significant about the plant's life cycle. So the point is, we can just observe our mind in that way but unless we use a conceptual framework to understand what is going on in the mind, we may become calmer, more concentrated, and perhaps even more aware, but it is unlikely to give rise to a depth of insight into the human and sentient condition.

In the term, "Abhidharma," *dharma* means "elements," which in this context means "mental and physical elements." It does not directly refer to Dharma teachings[23]. Understanding the elements and how they work together is what "understanding the dharmas" is all about in Abhidharma. The word *abhi* means "to make obvious." So Abhidharma means "making the hidden dharmas, or mental and physical elements of our experience, obvious." The idea here is that in our current state of mind, we are not intimately aware of all our mental and physical elements. As mentioned, we tend to lump it all together as solid entities. The Abhidharma approach pieces apart our experiences. This, in turn, gives rise to insight into the different elements and how we experience things, thus providing us with greater understanding of how our mind works, and how we can work with our minds in meditation.

For example, with regard to consciousness, Abhidharma speaks of six forms of consciousness; at other times eight forms are referred to. The six forms of sensory consciousness are visual (eye), nasal (nose, olfactory), auditory (ear), tactile (body), and taste (tongue, gustatory)—relating to the five senses—and what is often referred to as "the consciousness of consciousness" or "the element of consciousness," (Conscious Mind) which remembers and which anticipates future events.

How the sensory consciousnesses operate is an extremely important process to understand as it has a significant impact on the way we experience our emotions. Then, in addition to the primary consciousness, there are "mental events" or "mental factors," called *sems byung* in Tibetan. Since many different mental events are mentioned in Abhidharma, we will concentrate on those relevant to our discussion on grasping, fixation, desire, and emotions related to both positive and negative states of mind. So first I will lay the ground for this discussion.

Through the practice of meditation, we learn how the primary mind is supported by the mental events or mental factors, or sems byung[24]. The sorts of factors at work and which support the collection of the six sensory consciousnesses, or what is called "primary mind," determine whether we experience negative emotions like anger or jealousy, for example, or whether we experience positive emotions. The practice of meditation then is performed in order to work with the mental events so that we can transform ourselves.

As discussed in Part 1, it is important to note that meditation is not about learning how to overcome the experience of feelings and emotions such as desire altogether. It is about being able to distinguish between states of mind that lead to healthy experiences of emotions and mental events, and states of mind leading to unhealthy emotions and mental events. Unless our emotions and mental events are understood and dealt with, we can inadvertently continue to support negative states of mind and therefore encourage the negative emotions to grow.

That is why experiences are described in two ways. The first describes negative emotions as supported by negative mental events and, in the other case, reference is made to positive emotions being supported by positive mental events. However, positive emotions may be classified as either "defiled positive emotions" or "pure, non-defiled positive emotions." So, of course, first we develop positive emotions which are defiled, before we can experience completely non-defiled emotions[25].

Whether positive emotions are defiled or not is determined by the sems byung—mental events. Often positive mental events become intermingled with negative ones. In other words, when we try to transform our mind, it does not transform stage by stage in a very clear-cut manner; rather, different elements of the mind are becoming transformed.

Some of the negative mental factors that support negative emotions include being resentful, disinterested, untrusting, suspicious, covetous, and miserly. We may be able to work with and begin to overcome some of these mental events, while others may continue to occur without being worked with or reduced. Even if we are not working directly with particular negative mental events, we can be developing certain positive mental events to reduce the strength of the negative mental events we are working with, and the negative mental events we have not yet turned our attention to. For example, one may develop a sense of trust, which is seen as a positive mental factor, but while one is developing that, one may not have been able to overcome or reduce a sense of resentment. Resentment is seen as promoting the primary negative emotions including excessive desire, anger, jealousy, and envy.

If we had this understanding, we could develop the positive emotions we wished to, and overcome the negative emotions much more effectively than if we tried to tackle the primary negative emotions directly. So instead of trying to stop being jealous, envious, angry, and the like, we learn how to work with the underlying structure supporting the negative states of mind and emotions. In this way we will have more success. Although we may want to go straight to stamping out negativity when it arises, particularly if we feel we are being swept up in torrid emotional states, as we become more and more aware of the underlying negative structure that promotes such inflamed emotions, we will have more success.

This approach to working with the mind deals with each of the elements separately. The elements all connect with each other but each has independent characteristics in the sense that a specific negative mental factor, such as resentment, would support the growth of excessive desire, anger, and so forth. A mental event, such as malice, would support the growth of a variety of different negative emotions beyond resentment. Gradually, through meditation, we can learn to reduce or undermine negative mental factors while simultaneously developing the positive mental events that will support positive states of mind and emotions. We can then bring about real change and transformation.

So we need to think of our emotional states not as something that we deal with in isolation, through simply focusing on an emotion. Instead, to work with our emotional states effectively means we have to work with a variety of factors. We also need to include our physical state, in terms of our feelings, and interaction with other human beings. In other words, contrary to what we often think or believe, the emotions that we experience cannot simply be identified as being in the mind. The physical component is not to be denied. This means that our emotions are not simply just mental and our feelings or sensations are not simply just physical. Emotions are not something happening only in our own head, not just an intra-psychic experience. We have emotional experiences because of our interaction with others and the environment as well. It is extremely important to take all of these factors into account.

To reiterate, in understanding emotions, we have to recognize the various elements of our mental life and physical experience. Our mental life is supported by these elements. Without understanding them, we will not be able to understand our mind so well. Transforming our mind is not simply about transforming just one thing; it has to do with transforming the various elements. That is considered to be the approach that brings about final or full transformation.

Paying Attention to the Various Elements

First, we have to learn about the mental events and then through meditation we can develop more awareness of them. As we become more aware, we can more effectively deal with mental events in post-meditation situations as well. The Buddhist approach to transforming the mind has three aspects. First, we try to learn what the elements are, by reading and listening to appropriate teachings. Secondly, we meditate and reflect on such teachings. Thirdly, in post-meditation situations we try to think about these teachings so that we become more conscious in meditation.

Before discussing the mental events generally, we need to discuss "mental events that are always present when we have an experience of emotions," *kun 'gro lnga* in Tibetan or *pañca sarvatraga* in Sanskrit. Whether we have negative or positive emotions, the factors or events are always present.

The first one is "intentionality," *sems pa* in Tibetan or *cetanā* in Sanskrit. When we are angry, jealous, or whatever it may be, there is an object of anger—jealousy, and so forth.

Secondly, there is "cognition," *samjñā* in Sanskrit or *'du shes* in Tibetan. In this instance, it means one is making an appraisal of the situation. For example, we do not simply "get angry." We become angry because we sense that something untoward has been done to us; thus a judgment has been formed or made. This does not mean that one is engaged in some intellectual process, but rather an appraisal has been made of the situation or of the other person.

The third is "feeling," called *vedanā* in Sanskrit or *tshor ba* in Tibetan. There is a feeling component—pleasurable, painful, or neutral feeling. According to Buddhism, the feeling of neither pleasure nor pain is not an absence of feeling, but a distinct feeling, such as numbness. So feeling is also present, and "feeling" in this context refers more to physical sensation. It can be seen as accompanying emotion, as a component, but not an emotion in and of itself.

The fourth is "contact," *reg pa* in Tibetan, *sparśa* in Sanskrit. There has to be contact between our consciousnesses and objects. According to this way of thinking, it is not just the consciousness that is involved but our physical organs—sensory, auditory, or other sense organs—play their part in "contact."

The fifth is "ideation," *yid la byed pa* or *manaskāra*, is the final component, meaning that one has some kind of understanding and idea of what is happening.

From the Buddhist point of view, these five mental factors—intentionality, cognition, feeling, conscious contact with an object, and ideation—are present when we have any emotion. Each factor and event can be present in varying degrees of strength, so when the causes and conditions come together, they can manifest in a multitude of ways. Recognizing that these five mental factors or events need to arise together gives us some insight into how and why it is that we have an experience. In other words, certain things come into being because of causes and conditions, yet this does not lead to determinism. It does not mean that "because this happens, then that happens," in a very linear or causally predetermined way. There are many different elements involved and things do not always manifest in the same way. The net result can be different every time, due to the prevailing conditions.

This is very important to note, according to Buddhism, because from this viewpoint, the mind is highly prone to habituation. We have the idea of *saṃskārā*[26], for example, where we become conditioned quite easily and are then predisposed to react in a particular way. Habituation is not something that we can easily overcome, because habituation is a product of the various elements. According to Buddhism, habituation is perpetuated by varieties of existing causes and conditions and is not just a case of one thing giving rise to another.

If we are inculcated with the experience of negative states of mind and emotions, we become predisposed that way. We become habituated because of the many diverse elements at work. It is possible to overcome habitual tendencies by working with the different elements that contribute to perpetuation of the negative states of mind. While recognizing the persistent and compelling nature of our negative emotions, it should be noted that they can be overcome. If one works positively, using willpower, as discussed in part 1, while acknowledging the various elements responsible for causing perpetuation of a particular negative response, then that negative state of mind and the associated elements can be transformed. From a Buddhist point of view, negative habits are overcome or rendered benign, not simply through the use of willpower, but also through recognition and understanding. It is essential to keep this in mind.

From a Buddhist point of view, understanding emotions is important for meditation because we are seeking the two kinds of happiness, the distant goal of ultimate happiness that comes from attaining enlightenment, and the more immediate goal of reducing suffering and leading a happier life. To attain both kinds of happiness, it is important to develop positive emotions and states of mind because negative emotions and states of mind will never produce happiness. Meditation is one of the most powerful tools to develop a more sustainable happiness and a pliable mind, as it is through meditation that we can learn to work with the mind's different elements.

For instance, we calm the mind with śamatha or tranquility meditation to develop only some of the elements of our experience, the elements of concentration and awareness. These mental events are necessary for promoting positive emotions and positive states of mind. We need to develop other mental factors beyond concentration and awareness to work with all the elements. For example, "inattentiveness" is a mental factor that promotes negative emotions and states of mind so that is something we can counter. Therefore, once we develop some level of concentration and awareness, we should then make an effort to be more aware of other mental factors that reduce disturbance in the mind so that we are less subject to negative emotions.

Even though we may experience increased calmness, over time, through meditation, that does not mean we have overcome anger or jealousy. It means that our mind has temporarily become calmer. If a crisis or something drastic occurs, then the old negative emotions will most likely flare up, but developing a calm mind is still seen as necessary and essential. The Buddhist view is that if we have more understanding of what makes our mind agitated and disturbed, we will then have more chance of overcoming those negative states, hence the importance of understanding Abhidharma.

If we do not understand the dharmas, the various elements that perpetuate our mental life, are not even noticed. When we have more understanding, the dharmas become more obvious, they are easier to work with, and we have a better handle on what is occurring in our mind.

Chapter 11
Piecing Apart the Human Experience

There is a tendency for some people to associate Buddhist meditational practices only with śamatha or meditation of calmness, and they wrongly assume that if we learn to calm our mind, the disturbing emotions are going to disappear. This often helps fuel a misconception that what Buddhists say about emotions, and negative emotions in particular—is culturally specific and may not be relevant to a would-be meditator. It is not uncommon for a person interested in meditation to think, "what is important to me is just knowing how to calm my mind," and then skepticism can develop when it comes to detailed considerations about the human condition.

However, in Buddhism, having knowledge about the mind and our emotions has a direct bearing on our practice. Calming the mind is not going to make our troubles vanish as I mentioned in Chapter 10. Yes, Buddhism emphasizes the importance of śamatha meditation. It is important, and has become extremely popular in the west, just like *hatha yoga*. Such practices can have a positive impact and even help one face the world more heroically.

Nonetheless, this is not truly the Buddhist answer to how to transform the mind. If there is to be no real transformation, simply being able to calm ourselves down does not mean we have changed to any great degree. What we are seeking is not a superficial fix-up, but deep underlying change. Having a calm mind is extremely valuable, as mentioned in the last chapter. We are then in a much better position to look into how our mind works. The Abhidharma is an ancient text but the insights contained within it are not archaic notions of how the mind works. Living in the 21st century, we may believe, with the advent of western psychology, that we have everything that we need to know about the mind and that such knowledge supersedes earlier theories such as those contained in Abhidharma. I suggest there is room for both western and eastern philosophies and psychologies.

When people place emphasis on śamatha meditation and not on vipaśyanā, or insight meditation, it is often due to focusing solely on cultivating awareness—and it may only relate to teaching the person how to be in the "here and now." Vipaśyanā or insight meditation is about truly noticing what has come up in the mind while meditating, since it is extremely important for us to also *understand* what arises.

We could call Abhidharma "the standard psychology of Buddhist meditation" because it emphasizes how different factors and elements create any emotional or conscious experience. Being conscious or having consciousness is contingent on varieties of factors. There are many mental states within us that we have to recognize and then learn to transform. If we want to transform our mind, we have to recognize these mental factors and take them into account.

Abhidharma has been presented in the west for some time but it is only relatively recently that a strong interest in Abhidharma has emerged. I think part of the reason is because Abhidharma is often presented in a very succinct and condensed manner. It may seem abstract in this form and so we may not relate it to our experience easily. Normally a teacher is needed to unpack it and, with their commentary, bring the condensed version to life. This is true of many Buddhist texts. A text in its original form is not meant to be read as a book that explains everything, because in the traditional Buddhist setting it is assumed that there will be a teacher to explain it to those interested in following it through with practice and study.

In the previous chapter, I spoke about mind and mental events and explained that in Buddhism, according to Abhidharma, if we want to learn how to deal with our emotions, we need to understand the primary mind and then the so-called "secondary mental factors." If we want to understand emotions, we need to understand the primary emotions and the secondary emotions. This means that, according to Buddhism, we have the notion that the mind is like an organization and the mental factors are like the different subsidiary departments.

The Many Elements of Mind

Buddhism, more than other religious and philosophical traditions, emphasizes that there is no such thing as a unitary "mind." To reiterate, mind has many elements, and all of the elements have a specific function to perform. The reason we have conscious experiences is because these elements perform their specific functions—when they function together, we subsequently have the experiences that we do.

When we are confused and in the deluded state known as "samsara," we have a whole host of mental factors working together in a particular way and that produces the delusory samsaric mental experience. When we become more awakened, there are other sets of mental factors or events that come into effect to produce the experience of enlightened consciousness. In other words, overcoming the delusory samsaric mental state is not about overcoming a single thing called the "samsaric mind." There is not something called the "samsaric mind" that we can get fixated on myopically. To think that there is one thing called the "samsaric mind," according to Buddhism, is brought on by ignorance, through not knowing the mind itself. So, learning what sorts of dharmas we need to reduce, monitor, modify, improve upon, or cultivate, would determine whether we are being successful or not in terms of transforming our mind. As mentioned before, both positive and negative mental factors are called "dharmas."

Primary Mind—6 Elements of Sensory Consciousness Experience

So the primary mind is emphasized in Buddhism, which in itself is not unitary, because we have the sense consciousnesses: visual, nasal, auditory, tactile, taste, and consciousness of consciousness. Sensory consciousness is called *dbang po* in Tibetan—and it also refers to "sensory conscious experiences" or *indriya* in Sanskrit, meaning "power."

In the west, when we think about the senses, we think about them as being passive. Things are coming at us and the senses are simply there taking in the information. However, the term, "sense powers"—dbang po or indriya—means the senses are active. They actively engage in the world and organize the experiences that we have in life into types of responsiveness, such as aversion and attraction, and into categories, types, and so on. They organize and respond to what we see, smell, hear, taste, and touch. It is not merely what comes in, that impacts on our sensory apparatuses, but it is also how the senses themselves are constructed and in addition, the mental events or mental factors that determine what one experiences.

Conflicting Emotions—Primary and Secondary

Now we will look into some of the essential mental processes or factors that issue from the mind, sems byung, in Tibetan. When we discuss the emotions, we are talking about "something that issues out of the mind. In that respect, there are two sets of mental processes. One set involves the negative mental processes tied up with the primary negative emotions and negative mental substructure, which are called "primary negative emotions."

The second set of mental factors or mental events refers to the subsidiary or secondary subsidiary emotions, *rtsa nyon* or *mūlakleśa*. Mūlakleśa (Sanskrit) means "root emotional affliction": *mūla* means "root," kleśa means "emotional affliction," and *upakleśa*, or *nye nyon* (Tibetan), means "subsidiary" or "secondary conflicting emotions."

We have six mūlakleśa and twenty subsidiary or secondary kleśa or afflictions. In this chapter, mūlakleśa will be discussed. The upakleśa will be discussed in subsequent chapters, and we will consider the counterpoint to the negative afflictions.

As the Buddha said, "Dharma is like medicine, and what we suffer from is like a disease." We first have to identify which disease is causing our suffering, and only then will we be able to treat that disease using the appropriate method of healing.

6 Primary Conflicting Emotions—Primary Causes of Mental Afflictions

The primary mind was discussed in the previous chapter. Also discussed were the five omnipresent mental factors. We will return to these five intermittently as we go along, but first we will consider the primary conflicting emotions. Traditionally, there are five primary conflicting emotions, but in this instance we have six, which are excessive desire, excessive anger, excessive pride, excessive jealousy, being opinionated or dogmatic, and excessive doubt. These are called "the primary causes of mental afflictions," *rtsa nyon drug*.

We can see immediately that some of the behaviors listed have little to do with emotions, as we understand them in the west. For example, what does having doubt or being opinionated have to do with excessive desire, anger, or jealousy? To put it very simply, according to Buddhism, this means that as human beings, our thoughts have more power than our emotions. We are not like animals—with all respect to animals—because when we experience rage, anger, and disturbing emotions, our reactions are based on misconceptions—distorted ways of thinking which are at the root of our experiences of disquiet, unease, pain, and suffering. "Having doubt" and "being opinionated" are also mentioned because they are closely related to "absolute skepticism" and "absolute certainty," which go along with our experience of desire, anger, jealousy, and other conflicting emotions. Both absolute certainty and absolute doubt can inflame all of these emotions.

When we feel absolutely certain that an individual is mean or evil, even if they did not actually intend to do anything mean, simply due to our conviction, negative emotions may arise. If something wonderful happens, because we are skeptical, unsure, and harbor a general sense of doubt, we may be unable to embrace the joyousness of the occasion. Instead, we may remain in disbelief that something could be so wonderful. We may be concerned we are being duped, and so we assure ourselves of the importance of using our rational mind. Through entertaining such thoughts and mental processes we can miss many wonderful opportunities. Because of our skeptical mind, when somebody is being nice, the other emotions of jealousy, anger, resentment, malice, and so on, may even arise. This is another very important aspect to think about in Buddhism, because in terms of our psychological make-up, equal emphasis and attention has to be put on the thoughts because they condition our emotions.

Our thinking pattern and the emotions we experience go hand in hand. Some might say that this notion is similar to cognitive psychology or therapy. It is to a degree, but it is not precisely the same. We are not saying that thinking clearly, rationally, or in a reasonable fashion—or even thinking in itself—is the primary factor in determining what experiences we have as human beings. Rather, it means that our cognition plays a very important role in shaping our experiences and, in some ways, it can be more significant than our emotions. So in the course of our meditation it is important to address this. It is not just the emotions that affect and afflict our mind, but the thinking patterns that we engage in are equally responsible for giving shape and form to our mental life and emotional experiences.

We may think that we have specific emotional experiences that are disturbing and need to be worked on. We cannot successfully work on those emotions if we do not look at the thoughts accompanying them. It is vital we accept that there is always distorted thinking in the background of a negative emotion and, in fact, we may find when we reflect on it more closely, that it is not necessarily in the background. This is the type of insight we need to gain through meditation. Once we have calmed the mind we can look more profitably at what is happening in the calmed mind and be less inclined to overreact and be prone to excessive judgment. When we look at what is occurring in the mind when we are feeling emotional, it is clear that thinking is truly at the forefront of our mental life. Even when emotions dictate our lives and cause us to act in ways we regret, there is always distorted thinking encouraging and fuelling those negative emotions.

20 Secondary Conflicting Emotions

With regard to the twenty secondary emotions, first I will survey those to be discussed and then I will examine several of them in more detail. This should create a map from the Abhidharma literature regarding the emotions.

Anger

The afflictive mental factors mentioned in relation to the secondary afflictive emotions have to do with anger. The primary emotion called "anger" is not a singular entity. Anger can be many things.

1. "Being in a agitated state" or "having a feeling of dislike," or *khro*

ba in Tibetan, which is similar to agitation. Anger can be supported by and give fuel to this restlessness of mind and the feelings of agitation and dislike. If there is some element of our mind that is agitated, restless, or feeling dislike towards an object, then anger would arise more easily.

2. "Resentment," or *'khon 'dzin* in Tibetan, is exemplified in a situation where we feel that somebody has done us wrong and we are unable to forgive them. If we hold onto that mental stance, we are open to the arousal of anger, as we have become unforgiving, and that may fuel dislike, intolerance, and the like. These responses may become habituated so then anger would tend to arise automatically. At first it may be just one person we cannot forgive, but then the attitude could infiltrate our mind and we might end up being an unforgiving person, period. That unforgiving nature can lead to being vengeful and seeking punishment for those we are angry with.

3. "Malice," has the attitude of always wanting harm to come to others. It is a different kind of emotion from the other two already mentioned, those being agitation and resentment. An angry person may be kind, but a malicious person cannot be. A malicious person always has the wish that terrible things will befall others, and not just those who are enemies.

4. "Excessive competitiveness," is an attitude of always feeling that we lag behind in relation to others, and we may think, "I'm not good enough," or we may feel not good enough generally, whether it relates to intelligence, looks, social status, or other aspects of life.

5. "Concealment," in this context, refers to being unable to face up to ourselves and reveal what we are like to others. It relates to us hiding what we think are our defects and shortcomings.

6. "Miserliness" describes a poverty-stricken mentality, which is the

opposite of a generous spirit. We are not able to share anything and are territorial and possessive, feeling that we need to hang onto everything we have and lack the ability to let go.

7,8,9. "Deception, *in relation to oneself, and using oneself as the reason for deception, and using others as a reason for deception.*" There are three mental factors that relate to deception; the first two are similar but have subtle differences. The first has to do with "deception in relation to oneself." Even if one does not believe oneself to be a particular type of person, one wishes to project a certain image to others. So one deceives others by pretending to be someone one is not. The second mental factor related to deception is "using oneself as the reason for deception." Here, one promotes oneself to be a particular kind of person. It is not about what people think of one, but rather, what one thinks of oneself. Other people are at liberty to think an individual is either horrible or great, but that is not the question. The question is, while recognizing that we are not as people believe us to be, we still go ahead and pretend to be something else. Deep down we know that we are not that person. This is a form of deception called *gyo* in Tibetan. The third type of deception is "using others as a reason for deception," *sgyu*, in Tibetan, relates to us not thinking about how others may be harmed by our deception. It means that, for example, we can see an opportunity to make a lot of money, or be accepted in certain social circles, and we employ that deception without thinking about how it might hurt others in the long run.

10. "Representing oneself," *rgyags pa* in Tibetan, has to do with conceit; we believe we are a particular type of person, irrespective of what other people may say or think. We are not willing to move away from that fiction of who we believe ourselves to be.

11. "Wanting to cause harm." This attitude is present when we have a compelling need to make things difficult for others. We may want

to make sure things go wrong for others and then watch while they suffer. When we wish harm to others, and difficulty befalls them, we may think that somehow that will improve our quality of life.

12. "Shamelessness," *ngo tsha med pa* in Tibetan. This means we may have no conscience regarding our thoughts and actions, and how they may be affecting others. Shamelessness in itself is a secondary negative emotion. From the Buddhist way of thinking, a feeling of shame that is relevant, legitimate, and appropriate to the circumstances is beneficial. A feeling of shame can be seen as an opportunity to review our thoughts and actions and seek to do better. If there is no shame, such thoughts of betterment are unlikely to arise.

13,14. "Recklessness" has two forms. The first form is *"recklessness or shamelessness in relation to others,"* khrel med pa in Tibetan; and the second one, *ngo tsha med pa*, is *"recklessness or shamelessness concerning oneself."* It is comparable to the Christian notion of having no conscience—we have done something terrible, cheated somebody out of their fortune, for example, and we have no qualms about it. The second one has to do with *"being reckless and not caring what other people think,"* doing whatever one wants to do. This is to do with poor behavior—acting out in the most atrocious manner, without considering what others will think and how they will judge us.

According to Buddhism, it is better to address an issue, rather than find an excuse. If we feel we have done something shameful, it is best to take it on board and resolve the matter as much as possible within ourselves and if possible, with others. We need to forgive ourselves with the attitude that we will try to do better in the future and, when possible, offer a heartfelt apology or something similar, to whoever has been affected. Then it will be easier for us to move on. This is seen as a better approach than finding an external cause, such as blaming the other person for making one feel ashamed.

15. "Being untrusting" or *"not having faith or conviction."* In Buddhism, this secondary emotion has many implications. Not trusting the things that we have every reason to believe in, in terms of our belief systems, and believing in that which we should not have trust in, can be a great loss to us personally. It also refers to not believing in the people who we should believe in and instead, believing in others who are unworthy. For example, if we did not believe in His Holiness the Dalai Lama and his teachings and conduct, it would be a great loss to us personally. On the other hand, we may choose to believe in and give excessive trust to someone we barely know and whose values may not be clear to us. For example, with all respect to the financial advisory profession, we may go to a financial advisor or someone similar, for investment advice. They may paint a "too good to be true" investment strategy for us. We may have just met them and know little about them and then, having followed their advice, we experience significant damage or financial losses.

Conversely, not believing in the people who *should* be valued can land us in despair and even the development of a nihilistic attitude, if we then feel as if nothing matters. Having a commitment to certain values assists us in maintaining a high standard of conduct so we are not easily swayed or tempted by things that appear to be easy or pleasurable, but which may diminish the quality of our lives. We can believe in values that transcend our individual lives and, from that strong position, make beneficial decisions at any given time, based on those values and in relation to circumstances. In this way we do not have to rely on religious dogma or fundamentalism.

So it is imperative that we have trust. If we did not trust our friends, spouse, or children at all, we would not be able to live well as human beings. We are not necessarily referring here to "trust" in every respect and in every circumstance but rather, what is being referred to is an underlying *appreciation*. This does not mean we have to be credulous or gullible—that is one extreme. As modern or post-modern people, we may have a tendency to shift to the other extreme, where we doubt everything and do not trust or respect anything. This view can be seen as very blinkered. It is important to remember that everything is relative to something else, no matter what it is. Whatever is relative to another thing cannot, in itself, be absolute or right. Whatever is relative to something else must also be relative to other things as well, ad infinitum. So painting the world with one color as if all is doomed, misses what is possible and enriching. A fundamental sense of trust allows us to have faith and confidence in ourselves and in how we manage ourselves in the world. It allows for a plethora of experiences to be embraced.

16. "Being unmotivated or uninterested." *Le lo* in Tibetan, means "not thinking anything is significant or worth doing," that there is no point. So apathy, lethargy, and complacency are included in that notion of le lo.

17. "Forgetfulness," *brjed ngas* in Tibetan. Forgetfulness can inflame our negative emotions. When we do not pay attention, after a while we become so habituated that we have to look back to see what we actually experienced. As a result, while something is happening, we are quite unclear as to whether it is good or bad. This promotes the frame of mind that is conducive to the arousal of negative emotions.

18. "Stupor and mental agitation." While "stupor" refers to feeling psychically and mentally dull, "mental agitation" refers to when the mind is exceedingly active and agitated.

19. "Fixation," discussed in part 1, is a mental factor which prevents us letting go of what we have experienced conceptually, and then getting fixated on it or obsessed with it.

20. "Distracted mind." When the mind is scattered, it is because we have not learned how to discipline or put order into how we think and feel about things. This distraction is not simply brought about by scattered thoughts, but it also has a lot to do with diffused emotions and feelings.

Recognizing How Mental Factors Work Together To Understand the Mind

According to Buddhism, these mental factors work together to produce the negative emotions we experience. If we do not want to have these experiences of negative emotions, then these mental factors are worth paying attention to. In this way, we can more easily identify what is happening in our mind so that we can work with it more effectively. Instead of thinking, "I should overcome jealousy," "I should overcome pride,"—we can instead directly pay attention to and work with the mental factors supporting the underlying structure of that negative state or frame of mind, to more successfully transform ourselves.

It does not require excessive effort to be a little more generous, a little less malicious, and more attentive or forgiving. There are many scenarios that can help to illustrate this point. For example, if we invited a friend out for dinner and it came time to pay the bill, we might expect our friend to pay it, but in fact we could offer to pay for the meal ourselves. We can be less malicious, not just in terms of monetary value, but also with space, time, and advice. Further, instead of wishing people harm, we can begin to think well of others more often and wish them the best. If we hear good news about someone having recently been married, we can think, "I really wish that they will be together and happy for a long time," instead of being nasty and thinking, "I've been married three times and it was hell. I hope they will experience the same hell that I went through."

What is our Underlying Worldview?

What I am referring to here is an underlying attitude or worldview. As human beings, even in our unreflective mode, we have a worldview. Each of us sees the world in a particular way. This approach is about learning to adopt a worldview that will enhance our lives. When we learn to see things in a positive way, we can then see more possibilities and will not always habitually view things in the same old way or in a negative way. The Buddhist view is that, while not ignoring the difficulties of ourselves and others, we will be able to see how to harness our positive energies and willpower in order to transform ourselves and, through positive action, improve our own and other people's situations. According to this perspective, negativity will never lead to positive results.

If the compassion we feel for people living in great poverty is overshadowed by anger towards the people we feel are responsible for their plight, we can disproportionately experience more anger than compassion. That is why we need to build an understanding of the positive and negative substructures and the frame of mind required to slowly work with the different elements and gradually transform ourselves. It is not about stopping anger *per se*; rather, it is about what can be added to lessen the effect of the negativity.

Sems byung, means "something that issues out of the mind," as previously mentioned. What we cultivate involves both the existing structures in place, and the introduction of new ones, additional to those existing structures. With this approach we do not have to totally dismantle the old structures before we put aspects of the new structures in place. That is how one can become more kindhearted and less malicious, but have a scattered mind, yet still be making progress.

Through meditation, we begin to discover which of our shortcomings we can immediately address and which negative tendencies we can address later. It is important to know that this type of approach is acceptable. First, we can focus on the negative habits we think we can begin to change, such as becoming less stingy. If our tendency to be malicious is more deeply entrenched, we may need to delay more thorough work on that. In any case, being more aware of that tendency has begun the process of change in a less deliberate way. So we can begin where change is more accessible and can arise more easily. For example, we can look at being a little more generous, if that comes more easily to us. We may have an overwhelming attachment to material goods, but if we also tend to be somewhat unforgiving and we think that learning to forgive would come more easily, we may choose to leave the work on our inveterate, grasping tendencies till a later time. Then when a vindictive thought arises, we can say, "Okay, well, no big deal. It's okay." That is the Buddhist view. In that way, we gradually erode more and more of our negative tendencies by introducing positive mental factors using our willpower, as discussed in part 1.

I am sure we can all recognize the range of negative mental factors within this chapter. They may be very familiar to us all, yet, at the same time, we are all different people. According to Buddhism, we differ from each other because not everyone displays these mental factors to the same degree of intensity or in the same proportions. These qualities, states, or propensities are unevenly distributed and embodied in each samsaric individual differently so will manifest diversely and in a myriad of ways.

Chapter 12
Compatibility between Meditation Practice and Theory of Mind

Desire, emotions, and meditation are topics of great importance because otherwise, we could practice Buddhist meditation but without attention to the psychology of meditation, and our progress could be slowed or stalled. Traditional Buddhism uses psychological concepts in order to not only understand the mind, but also to understand meditational practices. Whether one agrees with this particular psychology or not is another issue, but it is best to pay attention to it and develop an understanding so that one can gain the most from the meditational practices.

When we study and do Buddhist practices, we need to understand these ideas and practices from the point of view of the traditional meditators who developed the explanations because the texts describe the insights they gained, while also capturing their thoughts about the practices. By looking at the ancient and traditional teachings—and specifically the techniques and concepts those practitioners used to deepen their understanding of the mind and the human condition—it not only gives us insight, but also sheds light on what the traditional practitioners encountered in their own practice.

As a side note, I want to caution that some practices are very formulaic and it is possible to become caught in the detail. It can become an obstacle if the appropriate intention and understanding is not integrated into the ritual side of some practices. However, when we are looking at the human condition and trying to recognize that which diminishes us and that which enhances us in terms of our spiritual growth, then developing our understanding of the mind is extremely important. It is crucial that we explore in depth Buddhist psychology if we wish to reap the positive rewards that this particular view, perspective, and approach can provide.

It is not the case that practicing Buddhism in the traditional way is unworkable in modern society. We could use such things as western psychology and other means to support our Buddhist practice, although that may not be necessary. Buddhist practices can stand alone, especially when we have a clear notion of what we are trying to do. That is why it is essential to study Buddhist theory thoroughly, and not just meditate. These two, theory and practice, must always go together.

If there is no compatibility between the practice and the theory, especially if we use a completely different theory, we are unlikely to get a good result. There has to be compatibility between theory and practice. We will receive more benefit from the practice if the theory is compatible with it, and supportive of a positive outcome.

Abhidharma teachings are followed in order to assist us in understanding our mind and the way it works in different contexts, such as during meditation, in ordinary day-to-day situations, when there is social interaction with other human beings, and so on.

Two Systems of Governance

So far in part 2 we have looked at mind and mental events and how, in Buddhism, mind is not to be understood as just "one thing," but as having many components, aspects, and elements. In addition to that, we have explored the concept of what are called the "mental factors" or "mental events," and "subsidiary mental events" that are associated with the primary function of the mind. So our mental life, then, is described as involving two systems of governance.

First, we have the *primary function of the mind* that includes the sensory activities—visual, audial, nasal, etcetera. This also has two components, those of the physical and the mental aspects, "five omnipresent mental events," the primary, and the many secondary mental factors, those factors that support our negative emotions and states of mind.

It is very important to remember that these lists are like "mental inventories"; they provide a good description of the human condition and are very relatable. They are great reminders, allowing us to recognize different features of our mind—how our mind works, the sorts of mental activities that operate, what impact they have on our lives, and how they influence our perception of other people, ourselves, and our conduct. We can refer to them often and use them as contemplations and guidance within meditation, and when wishing to gain knowledge about how the mind works.

We may wonder why there are so many secondary mental factors that support negative states of mind and therefore arouse negative emotions. The list is comprehensive and includes emotions, feelings, thoughts, and elements that are related to our mental life. It is advisable that we become more educated, as we go along with our meditation practice; it will refine our ability to distinguish between the many emotions and to see how they arise. For example, it is important to distinguish khro ba, which means "the experience of the arousal of anger," from 'khon 'dzin, which is the aspect that prevents us letting go of anger. Many different kinds of anger arise as products of the secondary mental factors. These secondary mental factors associated with the subsidiary negative emotions come about because of a mixture of the primary emotions—thus, desire and jealousy or desire and anger become mixed, and there are innumerable combinations.

The combining of primary emotions produces the secondary emotions. For example, we can distinguish between the first two forms of deceit. There is a considerable difference between g.yo, which is "deceiving oneself," sgyu, which is "deceiving another person," and "deceit involving hiding one's shortcomings." In the Abhidharma literature, we are not speaking about other people's perceptions of what we think we are hiding or not being straightforward about. What we are attempting to work with is what we ourselves are unable to acknowledge. There may be a suspicion already present, an acknowledgement of having this kind of negativity or that kind of negativity. It can be difficult to see ourselves clearly and it can also be difficult to fully acknowledge our shortcomings. Equally, we may acknowledge an issue we have with anger or some other factor, but our consideration of what is wrong may be misguided.

In other words, there is a lot of complexity involved. We may be hiding an aspect of ourselves from others that we do not need to hide because in our estimation we have exaggerated how bad the situation is. We may be ashamed and feel we should not allow anybody else to have knowledge of a particular shortcoming. Subsequently, we go out of our way in order to appear totally different from who we really are and what we are experiencing.

Then there is the situation where we deliberately try to deceive others. This is not about hiding what we believe to be our own shortcomings, but has to do with the deliberate intent to deceive. A traditional example is of an individual with a very low opinion of someone and yet they praise that person simply because they think they will benefit from a favor. In order to gain a favor or get something you want, you may lavish false praise on them.

Buddhist Psychology and Meditation

As discussed, Buddhist psychology is intimately tied to Buddhist practice, specifically the practice of meditation, because it allows us to distinguish between different kinds of emotions and mental states. According to Buddhism, knowledge is what we need. Willpower is important, but our willpower can only accomplish something to the extent that the mind comprehends what is taking place. If we do not understand what is going on, our psychological make-up, the kind of person we are, and what our nature is like—although our willpower will serve us reasonably well, its ability to do so will be limited. That is why in Buddhism it is so important to build a detailed and intimate understanding of our mind.

Through developing that understanding, our ability to enjoy our lives will be greatly enhanced. This is because it has everything to do with learning how to let go, forgive, and get on with life. The emphasis and guidance in these teachings is centered on trying to avoid our constant external focus on others and what they have failed to do for us, on how our lives have been made a misery because of specific situations or people, and so forth. By reducing our mono-focus and being more inclusive of the breadth of our experience, we reduce our tendency to grasp, cling, and fixate. We are given back the reins to direct our lives in the way that we want. That is why understanding our nyon mongs, kleśa, which refers to negative forms of emotions, is helpful[27].

When we speak of emotions arising within the samsaric mind, these emotions are seen to include distorted forms of thinking and feelings—anger, jealousy, and the like, an amalgam of responses supported by the mental factors that then disturbs our mind. That then deprives us of the experience of happiness and joy. So in combination, the negative states of mind, negative emotions, and the primary and secondary emotions give rise to the disturbed mind. The definition in Tibetan is quite a long one but put simply, kleśa or nyon mongs is something that afflicts the body and mind, lus sems gdung ba in Tibetan. This affliction then has the effect of eroding our willpower and we become wearied, tired, exhausted—dka' las sam ngal dub in Tibetan. "Dka' las" means "tired," "exhausted," and "ngal dub" is "wearied" and "depressed." *Mi dge ba'i las bskul ba* means "when we become disturbed, these states of mind are motivating factors for engaging in unwholesome activities." So mi dge ba'i las bskul ba means "encouraging" and "motivating." *Rang rgud rab tu ma zhi ba* means "in our own character, we then become completely disturbed"—non-peaceful—*ma zhi ba*. That is the definition of negative emotion.

It afflicts the body and mind, makes us feel completely worn out and it turns out badly in terms of how we interact with others. The depression factor that is mentioned, *dub pa* in Tibetan, is very significant because when we experience negative emotions, then negative states of mind arise, and these collectively produce the depressive mind. If our mind is filled only with negative emotions, we become diminished and forlorn.

Combined Causes of Conflicting Emotions

Let us now discuss 6 fundamental causes of the conflicting emotions or negative emotions spoken of in Abhidharma:

First there is "the basis," "one's own physical embodiment, what type of individual one is," which has to do with the constitution, our make-up.

The second cause is "the intentional object of the emotion that has to be present." *Dmigs pa*, is what our mind is intent upon. This relates to the omnipresent mental factors that were discussed earlier. Our mind is always orientated towards an object. Whenever we have thoughts or emotions, it is always about *something*—which is called "dmigs pa"; the mind is intent on something, so there is a purpose to the emotional response.

The third cause is, "a sensory stimulation that produces the emotions," *du 'dzi*, is the stimuli that are available. As human beings, our lives are very much based on our sensory experiences. We take what we experience through our senses very seriously. If we see something that we think is beautiful, ugly, disgusting, or revolting, whatever the case may be, we take our response seriously and as if it were real.

These first three—"the basis," "the intentional object of the emotion that has to be present," and "a sensory stimulation that produces the emotions"—are the most fundamental causes for producing human emotions.

The fourth cause is "discussing," *bshad pa*, that is, talking about things that will make us even more aroused, inflaming the emotions that we are already experiencing, talking about it, thinking about it, indulging in it. Always injecting whatever we say with emotional content. That emotional thrust is also one of the fundamental reasons we become extremely emotional. What and how we say certain things is in terms of the emotional driving force behind them.

The fifth cause is "habituation"—becoming habituated to a particular form of emotion; through myopic grasping and fixation we become predisposed to experience that emotion. It is both "mental and physical habituation." Buddhism does not discount the role of the physical in relation to the experience of emotions. We become habituated, both physically and mentally. Physically, we become accustomed to how we express ourselves—with certain gestures, gesticulation, facial expressions, and demeanor. It is there, of course, when it comes to physical behavior generally. Through a description of an individual's behavior, we can see whether they are peaceful or aggressive. It is contingent on this. That is the fundamental reason we become habituated; we get used to behaving in a particular way, both physically and mentally, and then can find it difficult to change. These latter points also apply to positive emotions; it is not just in relation to negative emotions. If we are behaving in a positive manner, it will then reflect in our demeanor, in how we project ourselves and behave.

The sixth cause is "thinking about," *manasikāra* in Sanskrit. "Yid la byed pa" in Tibetan—"thinking about it"—means thinking about what one experiences due to others: our past experiences, current experiences, plans for the future, and what we may experience in the future. It also means thinking about who has done what to whom, who has been hurt, who has been damaged, and so on. Thinking about all these, over and over in our heads, is also one of the fundamental reasons why we experience emotions in the way that we do.

Due to these causes, we then have the experience of the conflicting emotions. These causes are distinguished from what *gives rise to* or arouse our emotions. What gives rise to emotions and what *causes* emotions are seen as being different from each other.

Imprints and Hidden Triggers

With regard to the first cause, "the basis," when emotions arise, they leave imprints in our minds. These imprints then produce the *saṃskāra* that remain hidden. *Bag la nyal,* means "to remain hidden," or "latent." Emotions arise because we have not been able to overcome them through the practice of meditation. The second reason why emotion arises in our mind is because there is a trigger, an emotional trigger. So if it is lust, anger, jealousy, or whatever the response might be, there has been a trigger in close proximity, and so that emotion is elicited. The third reason is because we indulge in distorted forms of thinking. This, of course, is of great importance because, from the Buddhist point of view, we would not experience negative forms of emotion if we thought clearly and with accuracy. We suffer because we do not think well, because nothing we think about, which arouses negative emotions, is actually true.

This is very important because this means that if what we experience is "ultimately true" and undistorted, we should not suffer. If we have a real understanding of what is happening and are responding to things in a more immediate and realistic manner, in a genuine and non-contrived way, then we will not suffer. As discussed, as samsaric beings, our reactions are highly habitual, due to grasping and fixation. In life, we should be feeling good and thinking clearly, but we do not always have that experience because we think and see the world in a distorted way.

Discussion on Combined Causes of Conflicting Emotions Continues

The explanation for why emotions rise in relation to a given situation is that we react to a situation habitually because that emotional experience remains in an unresolved state. For example, with jealousy, if we have not resolved it, then jealousy can build up. It is very much alive. When the other conditional factors are met, which have to do with nyon mongs skye ba'i yul, "the object that would give rise to that particular emotion"—seeing someone as being better looking, more intelligent, or articulate than you—that allows jealousy to arise. The third cause is, for example, the reemergence of jealousy, which encourages that individual to become caught up in distorted ways of thinking. That way of thinking and reacting can become more and more entrenched. That happens when we further support our habitual reactions by convincing ourselves with ongoing personal dialogue, such as, "This person is not so great. Everybody thinks this person is so fantastic, so wonderful, but I can see they are not so great or wonderful."

When these factors come together, we have the experience of the primary and secondary negative emotions that we have been discussing. They arise precisely because of the primary causes, the fundamental causes of arousal of emotions, which have to do with *rten*, meaning the "basis"—our constitution, psychophysical make-up, or embodiment, that is "what we are intent upon."

"A sensory stimulation that produces the emotions," du 'dzi, on the other hand, has to do with the sensory experiences that give rise to emotions. When we see something beautiful, we immediately want it. We want to possess it, and then we cannot stop thinking or "discussing," it, bshad pa. Then it can be come ingrained, "habituation," *goms pa*. Therefore, there is a constant process going on in the mind—who we are and what attracts us, the presence of particular stimuli leads to emotion, which in turn leads to grasping or excessive desire, that stimulates excessive thinking and discussion, until the pattern of attraction/aversion is habituated—and this process consistently goes on in our mind, developing our character through this process.

From the Buddhist point of view and more broadly from a spiritual perspective, dealing with personal anomalies is not about dealing with our issues in isolation. Overcoming such things as excessive attraction and aversion, feeling victimized, the distorted ways we see ourselves and the world generally need to be addressed. This can best be done through building a more resilient and balanced "character." The use of the word character in this context is not referring to moral character nor is it referring to some kind of ideal type of person. From a spiritual or Buddhist perspective building character is about working with our body-mind complex to reduce our distorted view of ourselves and the world, and thus reduce our personal suffering. We can have a very dim view of ourselves unnecessarily so often. In fact some of the kindest, most caring, and sensitive people in the world also suffer from lack of confidence and low self esteem.

In this context "character" refers to our ability to accept where we are today, working with our weaknesses and delusions constructively without being excessively self critical. It is important to allow ourselves to be human, to seek help from others when we need to, and build realistic expectations of ourselves on the Dharmic path. That approach in itself can build strength of character. It is possible to see ourselves more clearly, and when we come across a weakness or a distortion within ourselves not to be devastated by it. It is best to smile at the imperfection, because acknowledging it is the beginning to working with it and the beginning of transformation.

We want to see ourselves more clearly and build a type of mental strength that retains the qualities of openness and honesty. Strength of character comes from this. This way of thinking about the mind and experience, how we apprehend the world can be seen as being quite different from how we think in more contemporary way.

Our samsaric mind tends to want to find the problem outside ourselves. We want to find out who is responsible for making us feel the way we do. We probe our unconscious and come to some kind of conclusion as to who implanted our emotional problem in the first place. We may think that particular individuals have to redeem themselves or apologize so that we can move on with our lives and really start living. The Buddhist approach, is the opposite of that idea. Character building is also about unconditionality, that we can move on with our lives even if there is no opportunity for "closure" as it is often called, with others. Whether someone redeems themselves or apologizes or not, we should still find a way to move forward. That is a very positive and transformative message.

That is why if we can take charge of our lives, it allows us to think in a more self-determinative way. Often, particularly in the west, we may speak about individualism, yet we so often talk about others—how others are making our life a misery and so on. There is complete incompatibility between the notion that one is master of oneself, and thinking that external circumstances are totally to blame. Buddhism says you can free yourself, so that no guru, husband, wife, father, mother, or anyone else, can have that type of power over you.

So it is an education in spiritual character-building. Buddhist psychology is about personal power. It is strength training for the mind, just like Lojong practice[28]. If we work with different parts of our mind effectively and consistently, then we can work with the mind as a whole, just like we do with our body. That is why, if we look closely at the different elements of mind, the different aspects of the mind, our mind will subsequently become stronger in the best possible and most realistic way.

We can work with what we are able to address and not fight too hard or struggle too much with that which we find excessively difficult to work with. That which can be worked with, and that which may be excessively difficult at the time, are interrelated. If we are having success working with one aspect of the mind, this will undoubtedly have a positive effect on other aspects. Eventually, even that which we find very difficult will become more pliable and workable. It is important to recognize this when approaching self-development in meditation. The approach should be gentle and realistic, and not focused on perfectionism but rather on the beauty and complexity of being human.

Chapter 13
Positive and Negative Mental Experiences

Throughout this book, I have emphasized the importance of understanding how Buddhism approaches human experience, what it says about desire, our emotions and habitual tendencies, and what we need to do in order to develop ourselves as human beings.

Historically, the psychology of meditation is taken very seriously and it is seen as an important part of traditional practices. What Buddhism presents is rich in theory, and it is an approach that we will most likely find resonates with our experiences. There is an objective and a subjective component to the Buddhist discourse on desire and our range of emotions. It is not based purely on subjective experiences, nor is it simply an objective description of the experience of having desires and emotions. Any discussion on emotions needs to be approached both objectively and subjectively. When looking at theories or approaches to understanding human experience, there can be a tendency to solely focus objectively, quantifying it all scientifically—or alternatively, to look only subjectively, the inquiry being based purely on feelings, so that the repertoire or range of human emotions is reduced to subjective experience. Without some degree of structure, it is easy to conclude, "When it comes to emotions, what I feel, what I'm experiencing now, is all there is to it." When considering the range of elements and causes that come together for an emotion or experience to arise, we can review and consider the complexity of human experience as both observer and experiencer.

So there are two sets of causes given in the Buddhist literature explaining how experiences such as negative emotions arise.

There are three reasons for "cause of arousal of a mental experience or emotion."

With the first reason, we generate particular kinds of desires and experiences because of our *vāsanās*, our psychological and physical imprints. Every time we have certain experiences, these do not simply arise and dissipate without leaving traces in the mind, but rather, certain propensities develop into habitual tendencies. This is often referred to as a response that leaves imprints or residue in the mind. Because of that, we respond, or a reaction is triggered, in a habitual way. These familiar patterns of response, such as suspicion, not trusting, or any from the range of emotional responses, arise when appropriate causes are present.

The second reason for "cause of arousal of a mental experience or emotion," is *nyon mongs skye ba'i yul nye bar gnas pa*, which means "the object of emotion." With negative or positive states of mind, when emotions arise, we experience them because we have a tendency to do so. This is simply because when we initially experience something it leaves imprints in the mind. However, in spite of that, we do not react to the emotion in the same way every time. This is determined by the vāsanās, the first cause of arousal of emotions. To use jealousy as an example—if a situation arises and an object of arousal is present with the potential for causing jealousy to arise, it would not arise habitually in someone not predisposed to being jealous. Jealousy arises when the object is there and the tendency to get jealous is already present.

The third reason for "cause of arousal of a mental experience or emotion," is "continuous indulgence in inappropriate ways of thinking," *tshul bzhin yid la ma byed pa* in Tibetan. So "tshul bzhin yid la ma byed pa" means "not thinking about the whole thing in an appropriate manner." Due to the vāsanās and by interpreting the object of emotion in an inappropriate manner, when we think about the object, we exaggerate the situation we encounter—that is, we make it worse than it is. For example, if we are jealous, we would want to reduce the person's qualities and attribute negative qualities to them that they may not possess. These are the reasons why negative emotions arise.

Positive Emotions and States of Mind

Positive emotions do not arise in that way, and this will be discussed in more detail later. What does apply to positive emotions is that if we have a positive disposition, we will then see a positive object of emotion in a more inclusive and less distorted manner, instead of in a highly distorted way, and will not indulge in excessively distorted thinking.

We will now briefly cover the positive emotions and positive states of mind. Before we do so, however, please note that in Buddhism, the psychology of meditation and moral or ethical psychology are intimately related. What Buddhism says about the psychology of meditation has implications in terms of our moral psychology because Buddhism does not simply talk about various mental states or our own personal experiences; it also notes the effects our inner mental states have on our interpersonal relationships.

There are eleven positive emotions and states of mind and they are as follows.

1. Trust

The first of them is trust, *dad pa* or *śraddhā* in Sanskrit. Positive emotions cannot arise if we do not have trust, if we do not trust anything. This involves not just trust in other people, but also includes trust in ideas, beliefs, principles, or ideals. Someone who does not believe in anything, does not respect or have any aspiration to cultivate ideals, and who is mistrustful of everything—in other words, a total skeptic, a nihilist—cannot develop compassion, love, joy, and other positive emotions well. If one has fundamental trust in other human beings, the natural world, one's ideals, principles, and as a Buddhist the infallibility of the Dharma and the omniscience of the Buddha—then one can experience positive emotions more comprehensively. If one does not espouse any principles and thinks everything is relative and as good as anything else, that kind of worldview encourages a nihilistic perspective. According to the Abhidharma way of thinking, that is an unhelpful view and attitude.

2. Shame

The second positive emotion is shame, *ngo tsha*. The feeling of shame, or *hrī* in Sanskrit, generally speaking, is seen as good. But of course, in Buddhism, we have to think about many of these emotions in terms of what is appropriate and also inappropriate. The appropriate experience of shame is a positive thing, however the inappropriate feeling of shame is not. Sometimes we feel ashamed of things when we have nothing to be ashamed of. For example, if a gang member feels ashamed because they did not have the courage to shoot a stranger in order to be accepted as a member, that is obviously inappropriate and even ridiculous, as many other feelings of shame are. However, not feeling shame when we should be ashamed is an example of being shameless, unfeeling, inconsiderate, and can suggest insensitivity. Shame is a good emotion when it is appropriate and it helps us to become a better person. It monitors our development and behavior and prevents us becoming reckless, which is one of the negative emotions. Recklessness is akin to doing whatever we like without care.

3. Decorum

The third of the positive emotions and states of mind is decorum, *khrel yod pa*, which is called *apatrāpya* in Sanskrit. Decorum, shame, conscientiousness, and "khrel yod pa," "ngo tsha" and "*khrel*" are interrelated; shame has to do with one's relationship with oneself. "Can I live with what I experience?" is what one should be thinking about. Before acting, one should be thinking, "Can I live with what I am about to do or what action I am preparing to take?" "Khrel yod pa" has to do with "whether others will accept me or not, if I go ahead and perform an act." Before one performs an action based on a feeling or emotion like anger or jealousy, for example, one should be thinking about "whether others would accept me if I went ahead and did these things." This is because Buddhism is about the well-being of ourselves and others. When we act in a reckless fashion, afterwards we suffer the consequences. So not only do we have to learn to live with ourselves, but we also have to live with other people, being our friends, family, and society at large.

4. Not Being Overly Possessive

The fourth one is called "not being overly possessive," *'dod chags med pa*, which is called *alobha*. *A* is negative, so it is like *med pa* in Tibetan. Here, it does not refer to "desirelessness" as some in the past have interpreted it. It means not being too attached to what we possess, so that if things work out, that is good, but if things do not work out, then we do not lose ourselves. So if we lose some of our wealth, our job, then we are able to learn to let go and move on.

It is also about reflection. To cultivate *prajna* or insight we need to reflect. We develop insight if we reflect on or think about these things. Reflection is part of the practice. When you reflect on something, you in some ways experience what is being presented and discussed. This helps our behavior to be in concert with the theory. Somehow we often have the idea that reflection and action are disconnected from each other—theory and practice—but reflection is not just about theory. Reflecting on life's essential experiences is an important part of doing what we need to do to live a healthy, wholesome life.

5. Non-Hatred

The fifth in the set is non-hatred, *zhe sdang med pa* or *adveṣa*. This encompasses all the things we discussed in the previous chapter about not being malicious or resentful. Positive emotion in Buddhism is the absence of negative emotion, so "zhe sdang med pa" or "absence of hatred" is an emotion in itself—it is the emotion of not having hatred. It is not just an absence, as we may think, but "zhe sdang med pa" is a positive emotion. It is the emotion of "not hating." What comes from that is a sense of caring, of wanting to be connected with and to help other beings—a loving nature can develop from that. As long as any subsidiary emotions connected to hatred are there, we cannot feel connected. We will feel alienated, dejected, rejected, and we will not fully believe or trust in anything, since all of these emotions are interconnected, a point which is most important to understand.

6. Non-deludedness

The sixth one is non-deludedness, *gti mug med pa*, or *amoha* in Sanskrit. This is the most important one. "Amoha," here, means "not understanding the dharmas," as we have been discussing—not understanding that there are many different mental states and propensities, attitudes, emotions, and feelings at work in giving rise to one single emotion. Our failure to understand the dharmas is demonstrated when we think, "I'm angry" or "I'm jealous," and "I can isolate this emotion or feeling." We do not realize that that particular emotion has arisen because of physical, mental, situational, and interpersonal factors.

7. Being Spirited

The seventh is called "being spirited" or "having the desire to energetically elevate one's attitude and understanding," *brtson 'grus*, also known as *vīrya*. If we want to overcome negative emotions, we have to have "vīrya," we have to have an attitude of wanting to do things, to engage and not become lethargic, complacent, despairing, dispirited, de-spirited, and so on. If the mind and the body have become very sluggish, then we are open to negative emotions and they will arise. The more time we spend not doing anything but indulging in more and more negative thoughts, emotions, and feelings, thinking, "Nobody cares for me, nobody cares. Everything is bad. I'm terrible"—the more lethargic and sluggish we will become, a victim of our own mental states. So, "brtson 'grus," or "vīrya" is necessary in order to rebuild our life in terms of positive emotions.

8. Conscientious Awareness

The eighth one is called "conscientious awareness," *bag yod pa*, or *apramāda*. We have to pay attention to our body, speech, and mind, how we go about things and conduct ourselves. It is about having sensitivity or intimate knowledge in regard to how we conduct ourselves, which is, of course, very different from being self-conscious. Here, it does not mean looking at what others are thinking, in terms of our actions, but paying attention to what we are doing, and how we are conducting ourselves, from our own point of view. If we do that, the positive emotions and mental states will arise. If we have no real knowledge of "how I'm projecting myself to others," even if other people tell us that we are behaving in a particular way, we may simply think these are their projections. But if we have the self-knowledge that comes from paying attention to what we are like, this will also go towards developing positive emotions and mental attitudes, adapting ourselves so that we behave more positively in real life.

To be conscientiousness about our conduct is a very important component of our moral or ethical upbringing or training, and also in terms of our psychological health and emotional maturity.

9. Processing of Body and Mind

The ninth one is processing of body and mind—*shin sbyangs* or *praśrabdhi*. When the more negative states of mind and emotions get a hold over us, we become very heavy in the body and the mind—mind becomes unruly, totally uncontrollable, and our body also becomes uncontrollable. That is the state of "being unprocessed," without "shin sbyangs." It is said we have to learn to lighten the body and mind so that they become pliable and workable. Often, our body and mind do not want to do what we want them to. By doing all the things that we have described pertaining to our states of mind, emotions, and so on, we can make the mind and body work more in the way that we want. This is an important part of developing positive emotions.

10. Equanimity

The tenth one is equanimity, *btang snyoms* or *upekṣa*. "Equanimity" does not mean we become inactive, passive or disinterested, but we have to have a balanced mind underneath everything so we can be more affectively engaged. Again, there may be some misunderstanding associated with this idea of "upekṣa," but it is in relation to our temperament—that we are basically even-tempered and not too excitable. It is a positive thing to avoid being too excitable. We can often get excited over negative things, rather than positive things. If we learn not to get too excited by our negative experiences, emotions, and states of mind, we will then gradually learn to put ourselves in a state of mind where these begin to perturb us less and less. Then the positive emotions can arise more easily.

11. Non-violence

The eleventh and final one is non-violence, *rnam par mi 'tshe ba* or *ahimsa*. Rnam par mi 'tshe ba means "not being violent." "Rnam

par" means "always" in Tibetan. It is "to always not be violent,"
which is not the same as "to not get angry." Our aim is to be "not
hostile"—not to be always thinking the worst of everybody and
everything, but seeing others in a different way, seeing people of
other cultures, religions, races, and those who are different from us,
without hostility. So "ahimsa" or "rnam par mi 'tshe ba" is the final
way of developing positive emotions.

Emotions and States of Mind

I think we can see that in Buddhism, negative emotions and
positive emotions are not something we can separate from negative
states of mind and positive states of mind. Emotions and states of
mind are related. States of mind are inseparable from the beliefs,
attitudes, and opinions that we have become habituated to. Unless
we deal with the whole—all the components of mind and
emotions—then we will not overcome negative emotions or
develop positive emotions. Negative emotions and positive
emotions cannot be isolated from the rest of the basic mental
structure or framework. In other words, we cannot work solely with
our emotions without changing our beliefs, attitudes, and behavior.
We cannot simply give rise to positive emotions if we do not take
all the influencing factors into account. If we work with ourselves
comprehensively and in accordance with these "eleven virtuous
mental states," as they are often called—then the positive emotions
will arise and negative emotions will diminish. Without that, we
could try to love every sentient being, but still be a horrible partner
at home for example. It is about attitudes and beliefs.

Many of the subjects we have discussed have to do with beliefs,
attitudes, and behavior, such as the attitude of not trusting.
Negative and positive emotions cannot be separated from our
beliefs, attitudes, behavioral tendencies, and dispositional
tendencies. All of these are causes that give rise to emotions.

In Buddhism, it is very important to understand what we are all about. We cannot be reductionist about the human condition. As Buddhism keeps saying, we have to walk the middle way. Managing our emotions, along with our beliefs, attitudes and so on, has everything to do with the middle way, rather than us first going to one extreme and then the other: the poles of eternalism and nihilism. Nor are we to demonize negative emotions as anathema and elevate positive emotions as supreme. The Buddhist view is to work with both of them so that gradually we become transformed. It is about transformation—working with what we do have and working towards what we do not have. To get what we want, we have to work with what we have.

Chapter 14
Buddhism, Psychology, and Psychotherapy

I have been emphasizing that meditation and developing emotional insight are intimately related topics. Sometimes though, we may think that in order to do meditation, we need to bypass emotions, so they somehow become detached. Meditation may be seen as a way to "tame the mind" but in this case "taming the mind" might mean developing a more philosophical and less dramatic response to emotional upheavals whenever possible. We may believe that through learning to concentrate and cultivate mindfulness and awareness in meditation, emotional afflictions we are subject to would disappear. However, this is not the Buddhist view.

With this in mind, I would like to talk a little about Buddhism, meditation, and psychotherapy—to articulate some of the crossovers and some of the differences. While I have read a significant amount of western psychotherapy and psychology and have been in dialogue with some of its clinicians, I do not consider myself an expert but I believe it would be useful to share some of my observations.

Some may choose to use psychotherapy or see a psychologist in conjunction with Buddhist practices, and personally I do not think there is a problem in doing that. However, I would like to make the point that for many, Buddhism is a total approach to life. There have been in the past and present some in the psychotherapeutic professions suggesting that Buddhism cannot address certain aspects of human life and human experience. It is a misunderstanding to say, for example, that psychotherapy can address aspects of life that Buddhism does not touch on. When one genuinely and wholeheartedly approaches Buddhist practice and study, and seeks the guidance of a qualified Buddhist teacher, the theory and how to apply it in a practical manner is given as a total path on how to manage oneself and approach all life's experiences.

When one is following that path in an authentic way, the experience of reduced suffering and increased happiness is truly available. The insight that develops provides one with the skill and insight to approach life's many challenges more skillfully. This ability can become more pervasive when it comes to improving one's overall state of being. This is true both in the short and long term. The process of reducing suffering and increasing happiness builds enormous resilience and can minimize the consequences of such things as trauma. Continuing on the path can lead to liberation.

A half-hearted approach to self-understanding and self-improvement will never reap significant results, whichever path we choose. If we shift from one discipline to another, not fully devoted to any one approach, our relationship with other human beings will suffer as well. Genuine commitment needs to be made within ourselves and an expression of proper commitment in relationship with others.

Some aspects of the Buddhist worldview might seem quite foreign or discordant to the modern ear. However, even if for some people, aspects of Buddhist theory do not ring true, those aspects should not be dispensed with too easily. It is not recommended to use Buddhist theory and practice like a smorgasbord, picking what we like and leaving the rest behind. What one leaves behind may be an essential tool for understanding the labyrinth of the samsaric condition. So our approach to theory and practice needs to be thorough and our criticism can be arrested for a time, curbing our tendency to discount the value of something too quickly before investigating it properly. This gives us time to develop a more thorough understanding. Then one is in a much better position to make an informed decision and debate the validity of many of the theoretical points. In Buddhism this is the more traditional approach, and is seen as far more valuable than launching in with too much criticism regarding aspects of the theory or practice before one has a good grasp of what is being presented. Further, gaining an understanding of how to apply Buddhist theory to its meditational practices will help us develop a deeper understanding of the human condition. We will then be better placed to address the dominant issues in our lives in such a way that immediate and long-term suffering can be reduced.

In many ways the modern person has been inculcated with relativist ideas and if we really want to follow Buddhist teachings and gain great benefit, it requires not only commitment but also a degree of conviction or faith—conviction in a reliable teacher and conviction born from experience and study. This is essential but not in a dogmatic or fundamentalist sense. We can commit ourselves to something without the need for discounting the value of other things. Equally, we do not have to be so promiscuous in terms of our beliefs and attitudes. It is helpful to believe in something and it is good to have a worldview, particularly if we look at the world with a broad perspective. A comprehensive outlook can be found in many approaches, including Buddhism.

From the point of view of Buddhism then, it is preferable that we do not approach life with too much inconsistency, haphazardly, or with a defused and distracted approach. I think that sometimes when people talk about Buddhism and psychotherapy that is exactly what can happen. A tendency can arise for some to cut

Buddhism, and for that matter psychotherapy into pieces, fitting aspects of it into their preexisting worldview. So if we are prone to making decisions about what is of value and to be adopted, and what is not of value and to be ignored, when we encounter a particular discipline, these value judgments can be made prematurely before we recognize or understand the value of what we have discarded.

Buddhism provides a comprehensive view, but we often risk evaluating our own progress on the path too narrowly and often too harshly. As a Buddhist or regular meditator we may think, "I get up every morning and do my meditation, and I have not changed—I still scream at my children, and I still get jealous." It is important to consider more broadly how we are progressing. It is easy to focus on the pieces of ourselves we are not happy with. It is important not to give all our attention to how far we have to go on our quest for self-improvement and self-knowledge. It is far more powerful to see how far we have already come. This type of appreciation and approach can install confidence, and provide us with a richer and more motivating attitude.

We may also think many aspects of Buddhism are culturally based and thus irrelevant to us, "This is Tibetan stuff," or "This is Japanese," "It is culturally bound and not relevant to me." That can be partly true but is not always the case. Still, our approach needs to be comprehensive and balanced between serious study and meditation practices. Abhidharma, the Buddhist theory of psychology, has always been a very important part of the Buddhist tradition. Without us developing understanding of this major aspect of the tradition, and further not properly addressing the breadth of Buddhist study and practice, this risks such profound teachings being lost, diluted, or even dismembered through not being properly integrated. Further, it reduces the transformative capacity this tradition can have on our lives.

Individualism and Relationship

Individualism and individuality are strong aspects of the western frame of reference and worldview generally. We have personal, interpersonal, and transpersonal, or super-personal relationships and perspectives.

In relation to our personal experiences of anger, jealousy, and so on, Buddhism does not emphasize the notion of going deeper into our experiences, asking such questions as, "Where does my jealousy originate from? Why am I so envious of other people? Why do I feel a sense of loss?" or whatever the case might be. From a Buddhist perspective we do not delve into questions like that. Rather, we recognize the issue of jealousy and then apply one of the many approaches that help diminish its effect.

Within the Abhidharma approach, one generates positive aspects of oneself that diminish the force of and focus on a negative experience such as jealousy. In Buddhism, the interpersonal aspect is very important. Even though we are not focusing on that which is diminishing us, that is not because the aim is to ignore it and hope it goes away, but instead, it is to educate ourselves on how to transform and manage difficult states of mind. It is about reducing the human tendency to grasp and fixate on a problem or a difficult habitual tendency. We want to loosen the grip our minds can develop on aspects of ourselves we and others find problematic. In that sense, rather than delving deeply to discover where a particular neurosis may have originated and becoming fixated on that as the cause of our misery, we look at disturbances that can be more easily detected and then transform those. In that sense, we are not digging down deeply but rather responding to what arises in our mind. It is about developing a more inclusive and broader view, rather than a myopic view of ourselves or a given situation.

In part 1 of the book, we addressed the notion of renunciation and to some extent, non-attachment. These are concepts that can be easily misunderstood, not only by those external to Buddhism, but also by those who consider themselves Buddhists. We discussed the notion of renunciation, concluding that such a decision is more about deciding how one wishes to spend their time, than it is about rejecting a conventional life. A monk or nun decided on the monastic lifestyle so that pursuits such as career, family, and mortgages and the like, do not distract them from their desire to study, practice the Dharma, and participate in other monastic activities such as service to others. Equally, a householder or layperson may devote their time and service to caring and providing for their family and others, which includes pursuing a career, generating an income to support the family, and so on. This is a different kind of service being offered to others and one's community. In both situations, however the practitioner, be they a monastic or householder, needs to work with the tendency to grasp and fixate. In so doing it is important to understand how the human mind works. This emphasis on overcoming our fundamental, samsaric tendency is so that we can reduce our propensity to apprehend the world in such a way that it causes unnecessary suffering. So if we reduce our myopic tendency to fixate on aspects of our experience, we will instead relate more comprehensively and inclusively to ourselves and the world. When we experience a great deal of suffering, it is hard to genuinely connect with others. By freeing up the mind from its fixations, we can reduce our suffering and enjoy life more, and relate more closely to ourselves and others.

The purpose of retreat is not to learn to detach ourselves from others and the world. Rather, the aim of retreat is to reduce distractions and devote time increasing our understanding of the human condition. We can then use that insight effectively to work on our habitually held beliefs and perspectives, in order to see the world more as it really is, rather than how we have personally constructed it to be.

We want to look at our fundamental tendencies of grasping, negativity, excessive desire, and so on and become more open to seeing the world as it exists without any contrivances. It is in that way we can start to recognize the interconnected nature of all things, and build a deep and genuine connection with and compassion for others.

Generally speaking, when we look at the notion of non-attachment in the context of the extended family unit, attachment to one's family has been a more significant issue in the east when compared to western culture. My experience growing up in the east characterized a long history of the extended family forming the center of one's world and worldview, whereas in the west, while family is important, it is often not as extended and encompassing. In that respect, non-attachment can be seen somewhat differently, dependent on cultural variations. None-the-less, the point to be made here is that relationship is fundamental to the Buddhist view, and is strongly tied up with ethical conduct. If we can release our attachment to the views that inhibit us and make us suffer, we can be more present.

Further, if any samsaric condition is all encompassing and does not leave room for spiritual practice, study, and personal growth, one may need to find some release. So one can see non-attachment in somewhat general terms, not being tied in too tightly to whatever lifestyle one leads, to have some time and space available to pursue one's spiritual goals, without shirking any fundamental responsibilities.

Tibetans, for example, value relationships above everything else, and that includes their relationships to their own teacher. It is actually not beneficial if relationships are not considered as valuable. It is all too common to see people throw away a good friendship because there has been a misunderstanding, or break up a marriage because it became a little uncomfortable. Of course, I am not saying that every form of relationship is good, but it is not a good thing to free yourself from a real and genuine bond.

When we are looking for enlightenment and self-realization, that does not exclude us from establishing ourselves as a person, in relation to others. Obviously, the goal of enlightenment is not about ending all relationships. The immediate goal, as we have discussed, is to increase our happiness in this life. Enlightenment is all about relationship, not being absorbed in one's personally constructed world but rather, being immersed in reality. To experience reality, "how things truly exist"—is the most intimate of relationships to have with oneself, others, and the world and such clarity is something that we have to work for, over time.

What we should be working towards is a sense of self-fulfillment that comes from gaining personal understanding about ourselves, which corresponds to our personal experiences. In a spiritual quest we are searching for some degree of personal understanding of ourselves. Guidance here is important so that our search is effective and reduces pain and suffering rather than increasing it. Those three—personal, interpersonal, and super-personal development—are described among the twenty adverse conflicting emotions and eleven positive emotions and the process of building positive mental states to elevate our personal experience.

Tension between Buddhist Values and Cultural Values

In our understanding of Tibetan Buddhism it is important to make distinctions between Buddhism and Tibetan cultural values—Buddhist values and Tibetan values do not necessarily coincide. Even though Buddhist values inform Tibetan values, nevertheless they are distinguishable—they are not the same. Tibetan values are just like western values, in that they are based on samsara. If we are really following the Buddhadharma, all cultural values need reevaluating and should be modified to correspond to Buddhist values. Within every society there will always be tension between the ethical thing to do from a Buddhist standpoint, and the right thing to do, according to the status quo of that culture or society.

This evaluation relates to how we should treat everybody and it relates to our own emotional well-being. The import of this is that we should try to treat everybody in the same way, drawing from the same attitude or ethic, while recognizing that everyone is not the same. This is important and can be complicated in terms of political and social theories.

From a Buddhist point of view, to try to treat everybody in the same manner is different from thinking everybody is the same. We are not all the same. Buddhism has a technique that involves treating everyone alike, which has to do with non-discrimination, but one still needs to be discerning on the relative, day-to-day level. The practice of treating all people alike has two main approaches: The first approach is to treat everybody the same while we are meditating. That means that we generate love and compassion for all beings. So when we are doing the four Brahmavihāra practice of loving-kindness meditation—then we see everybody in the same way. More specifically, in meditation we can use techniques, such as, thinking of someone we love dearly and generate love for them. Then we can think of someone who is just an acquaintance and generate the same intensity of love for them. Continuing, we think of someone we do not like or even hate, and we generate the same intensity of love for them within our meditation. In this way, our love can develop an all-encompassing, expansive, unconditional, non-discriminating quality[29].

But in everyday life, in post meditation, *rjes thob*, it is different. It is incumbent on us to treat everybody with a similar underlying attitude or to put it in other words, we recognize their Buddha nature or potential for enlightenment, while being skillful in relating directly to people. It is not an absolute but we need to try our best to develop and use skillful means and insight into the human and sentient condition, in order to treat people appropriately. We try not to discriminate against anybody because of their religious persuasion, their race, educational background, economic and social standing, gender or sexual preferences, etcetera. In other words, we avoid stereotypical generalizations both when we relate directly with people and within our meditation.

That is the Buddhist view, and it is imperative that we have an understanding, because we take this notion of equality so seriously. The fact that we are not all the same and thus not all equal is not the problem. It is challenging to treat everyone equally. That is the idea but, in practice, we know everyone is not equal.

Further, we want our children to go to a good school, we seek betterment, and we wish to elevate our lives and lifestyle—it is important to be honest about this. While pursuing a better life for ourselves, our family, and community, we can intentionally seek that for all beings. We can develop an inclusive attitude and want the best for everybody. It is always about elevation, and not about finding a comfortable level, nor is it about connecting by finding the lowest common ground.

From the Buddhist point of view, it is always about the other, and not about ourselves having to be treated equally. It is about treating others—the less fortunate—as being equal. It is not about us being treated the same as everybody else, which is often what we tend to be concerned with. In terms of oneself, one should always try to excel, without falling into the trap of thinking, "I'm special, I'm great, I'm wonderful," etcetera, because we are not. As samsaric beings, we are constantly making mistakes—misapprehending the world, grasping at certain experiences with excessive attraction or aversion, swinging from one extreme to the other, and so on, thus disturbing and disrupting the mind. We need to see desire for self-elevation; humility when we identify our shortcomings; confidence, when we recognize our potential; and the skill to effect significant change in ourselves—as being co-ordinates, not contradictions on the spiritual path.

So we clarify the mind through study and practice, and then, with humility, strive for our own betterment with kindness and diligence, and for the benefit of all beings. As I said, there is no contradiction when it comes to developing humility, striving for excellence, and concerning ourselves with the well-being of others—no contradiction. That is what Buddhism teaches and that is what it is all about. Emotionally, we will fare better if we think like that instead of getting bogged down by the emotional ideal that we are all equal. We do not want to slow down our own growth in order to be so-called "equal." The desire to elevate one's life experience is a far greater motivation than the idea that seeking to have a contrived sense of "equality" to others would somehow make us a better person. The misapprehension of equality can diminish our potential, in some ways, for the sake of wanting relationship, albeit, with a lower standard. Aiming for the lowest common denominator is never an expression of equality.

However, in the context of our aspiration for equality, to treat everybody the same way, free of prejudice, with skill and care, and at the same time wanting to excel—from a Buddhist point of view, our only real failure is when we choose one over the other. If we treat everybody well and ourselves well simultaneously, there is no contradiction. We will be able to form positive relationships with others in that way.

Traditionally, Buddhism has always emphasized the importance of relationships. As a further example, in Tibet, the monastic sangha go out into the villages as traditional doctors and healers, they provide guidance with problems—emotional, financial, or whatever issue it is—they care for the dying, perform blessings for marriages, homes, and newborns, and even the well-being of farm animals. They are a vital spiritual support in every aspect of the villagers' and nomads' lives. While there are some monastics in extended retreat, most are an important and integral part of day-to-day living.

We have all inherited our respective traditions and we think about things differently because of that. Buddha did not teach empiricism because of the simple fact that what we see we cannot believe—it is the opposite. What we see has to be informed by our conceptual categories, even rudimentary things like tables and chairs, let alone religious ideas, spiritual realization, and so forth. We cannot base everything on experience alone. We would be living very impoverished lives if we only believed what we saw. What you experience is not the most important thing, because we know that, from sense consciousness to ideas, we have been deceived again and again. Using a traditional example, we can think that we see a snake, but then we realize it is not a snake but a stick.

How many times have we been deceived by our senses? We see it and believe it—and the way we see it and believe it is mostly based on prior experience, developed opinions, and interpretations. We are deceived repeatedly, again and again. The way we see what we see lets us down all the time. That does not mean we should believe what we do not see or hear or smell or taste or touch. We do not have to go to the other extreme because, as Buddhism says, we should practice the middle view and the middle way. It sounds so simple yet it is very difficult to follow and practice.

We have to juggle all the time in life with the illusory and the real. For example, we have to negotiate between our conceptual categories and sensory impressions—we cannot trust our senses fully, but we cannot trust our conceptual schemas completely either. If we get too caught up in our sensory experiences then, through not really thinking clearly, we can become lost in the sense experience.

166 Desire: Why It Matters

One needs to focus on the senses as well as the concepts because emotions are attached to experiences on both the sensory and the conceptual level. So emotions are attached to the sensory experiences and the conceptual apparatus at work. From Plato to the present time, so often in western thought it is believed that if we conceptualize and think with clarity, our experience can be free of emotion. However, from a Buddhist perspective, as long as we are using concepts, there will be emotional elements generated and attached.

How we manage our emotions has to do with our worldview. It really comes down to that, fundamentally speaking, our attitude towards life. If we are Buddhist, then it is important to have a consistent, comprehensive Buddhist worldview on life rather than a piecemeal one. If we have a consistent view and remain open-minded, then when we deal with our life in that way we can find more balance. Our life cannot be in balance if we have a fragmented attitude towards life.

As samsaric beings, being fragmented is what we already are. We think about so many things, and value so many things, but in a disorganized way. So we have internal conflict and we are often torn. But if we have consistency and, for example, dharmic values[30], our thinking will be more organized. That does not mean one has to be a fundamentalist of some kind, or even dogmatic. We do not need to think, "What I believe is the truth," or "Only I possess the truth," or "What I believe is what everybody should believe." It can be difficult to avoid falling into being either totally dogmatic or totally skeptical. People fall into one or the other pitfall and do not realize that one should be focusing on not falling into either. Life is all about how to negotiate between those two extremes— between extreme skepticism and extreme dogmatism, and the immediate impact that has on our emotional well-being and that of others. The more dogmatic we become, the more emotional we become; and the more skeptical we become, the more emotional we become.

Chapter 15
Enrichment through Positive Emotions

Emotions have the potential to arouse us and intensify our experiences. Thus, from a Buddhist perspective, positive forms of emotion should be cultivated, not devalued; while with negative forms of emotion, we should learn to overcome the hold they can have on us. As I have discussed, negative emotions become less powerful when we generate positivity, so "managing our emotions" is not about stamping out negativity.

Buddhism teaches the importance of leading a life of equanimity, serenity, and peace. But that ideal may be misinterpreted. We may actually devalue emotions, as if the emotions set off imbalances and disturbances. There is no contradiction between leading a life of equanimity, serenity, and peace and finding fulfillment based on our own emotional experiences. This is where great richness can be found.

The reason for that is certainly not because negative forms of emotion serve our day-to-day experiences well, and positive emotions serve us well only in the distant future, in our pursuit of nirvana. On the contrary, positive forms of emotion, if cultivated properly, disempower negative forms of emotion. If we are experiencing any form of negative emotion, it means we are not happy or content. Negative emotions do not serve us well. When we experience feelings of jealousy, envy, or other forms of negative experience, it can set us off-balance; we can be degraded and experience disharmony.

Our thoughts and emotions are intimately linked. If we think with clarity, we will be able to enjoy emotions in a much more fulfilling way. Earlier in the book, I presented different forms of thoughts, attitudes, beliefs, and emotions. Thoughts and emotions create the substructure for intense emotions to arise. Often, within our lives, instead of thinking clearly and being emotionally rich, we have convoluted thoughts that give rise to negative emotions. Negative forms of emotion should be understood in terms of our negative thoughts, feelings, attitudes, belief systems, and so forth. These give rise to and fuel and refuel our negative responses, our negative emotions. In Abhidharma literature, the positive forms of emotion and negative forms of emotion are linked to the range of mental events.

Earlier, we discussed "relationship" versus "individualism." Generally speaking, both individualism and relationship are emphasized in the west, but relationship is emphasized more in the east. The concepts "relationship" and "individualism" are not necessarily compatible if we are unwilling to make compromises. Equally, societies that value relationship more than individualism still manage to incorporate diversity. For example, in India, sadhus sometimes wander about stark naked and yet there is recognition and respect for them as holy people. The question is, fundamentally, whether it is individualism or relationship that is valued: does the individual have an opportunity to express themselves? Spiritual practitioners as represented by Taoists, Confucianists, Buddhists, but also hermits, wandering vagabonds, mystics, crazy yogis, and so on, can be incorporated into an otherwise ordered and less individualized society, in terms of its values.

Fragmentation and the Deluded Mind

It is fragmented because there are many different elements simultaneously at work, or working in quick succession. We cannot understand our mind as being unified and simple, and separate from what is physical. Instead, we need to understand the mind in relation to the various aspects of our mental experiences.

In Buddhism, this is what is referred to when we speak of "deluded mind." Deluded mind is characterized by fragmentation because different elements of the mind are both working together and against each other. Sometimes there is harmony between and among the elements, at other times there is tension, and sometimes they are opposed to each other, which can introduce an intense experience of mental disturbance and pain into one's mental life. That description is how we should understand what is meant by our "mental life" and our "emotional life" in Buddhism.

So, apart from the positive emotions and negative emotions, there are other events at work in the mind, called *gzhan 'gyur bzhi*, which means "four changeable mental events." The four changeable mental events are states involved with sleep, regret, investigation, and analysis. These are also related to meditational practices.

We have already talked about the positive states of mind and positive emotions, and the negative states of mind and negative emotions. When we speak about states of mind, it refers to attitudes, beliefs, and the like, apart from what we would normally regard as emotions. Here, sleep, regret, investigation, and analysis are called "changeable mental states" because these states—sleep, regret, investigation, and analysis can be either positive or negative. For example, the state of mind when we fall asleep, according to Buddhism, we should take notice of. So we take notice of each state of mind, as it manifests.

Defining the Four States—Sleep, Regret, Investigation, and Analysis

1. Sleep

Sleep is called *gnyid* in Tibetan and *middha* in Sanskrit. It can be very powerful to consider the quality of our sleep and the process of falling asleep. We can ask the question, "Does sleep engender a positive frame of mind or a negative frame of mind?" Abhidharma literature says that we do not have to think of sleep as either a negative thing or a positive thing. It could be either, because the mind that goes into sleep follows from whatever mind states one has been experiencing during the day, so what one experiences during sleep is determined by extraneous factors, not just change to the state of sleep.

We do not just fall asleep. Our state of sleep is informed by or imbued with various experiences from outside that "falling asleep" state of mind, so it could be either positive or negative. Even while we are sleeping we can experience either positive emotions or negative emotions.

2. Regret

Regret is *'gyod pa* in Tibetan and *kaukṛtya* in Sanskrit. In the Abhidharma literature "regret" is classified as a form of emotion with the quality of a "changeable mental state" called gzhan 'gyur bzhi in Tibetan, which means it could be either positive or negative. So whether regret is considered a good thing or a bad thing depends on what we feel regret about. Just the feeling of being regretful without having a context cannot determine whether it is positive or negative. It is determined by the object of regret. That is why we regret certain actions, attitudes, feelings, or emotions, in relation to one external event more than another.

The positive or negative quality of our regret is determined not only by our response to the external event but also by our motivation and whether our motivation is appropriate or not. So, if we regret something appropriately, that is seen as positive. If we regret something with inappropriate motivation, that is seen as negative. For example, if we regret that we were unable to do serious harm to somebody, this is obviously very negative, but if we acknowledge that we went overboard in our reaction to somebody, this type of regret is considered positive and thus enriching.

3 & 4. Investigation and Analysis

Investigation and analysis are mentioned within the nine stages of śamatha or tranquility meditation[31], "investigation" being *rtog pa* in Tibetan and "analysis" being *dpyod pa* in Tibetan. "Rtog pa" is called *vitarka* in Sanskrit, and "analysis" or dpyod pa is called *vicāra*. Investigation has to do with looking at things in relation to the general situation, and analysis is similar to examination, as in "examining the body-mind complex in detail."

It is said that we overcome these four states through the practice of the nine stages of śamatha. We are not required to go through all the nine stages necessarily to transcend investigation and analysis. However, it is said that if we reach the highest state of śamatha, then reportedly we will automatically overcome investigation and analysis.

However, in the context of vipaśyanā or analytical or insight meditation, investigation and analysis are necessary instruments of meditational practices. So, again, it depends on what we are investigating and analyzing— rtog pa and dpyod pa. Investigation and analysis are important for building insight into how the mind works within vipaśyanā so it can be used in such a way that gives rise to positive responses and positive emotions. If the object of analysis and investigation arouses our negative emotions—jealousy, anger, envy, spite, covetousness, deceit, shamelessness, laziness, recklessness—all the things that were listed earlier in relation to negative states of mind and negative emotions, then that is not helpful unless we can encourage positive emotions through skillful investigation and analysis. So to summarize, investigation and analysis can be a good thing or a bad thing depending on our motivation and how these thought processes are managed.

Some people may think that using reasoning or intellectual exercises is anathema to meditation or to overcoming negative emotions or states of mind. If we have a comprehensive picture of the mind—a detailed map of the mind—and how it works, that will help in navigating the mind. It is actually something that we can see and relate to immediately. This analysis does not determine what the mind is like in itself, as that is much more intangible and elusive. It is easier and more useful to describe how the mind functions than it is to spend time speculating on what the mind itself is. When we know more fully how the mind functions we are in a better position to work with and manage the mind and there is much to be gained from doing that.

Knowing how negative emotions and states of mind arise, how they are encouraged and persist, and what we need to do in order to positively change them is of great benefit. We can learn how positive states of mind can be cultivated, and how to work with them to maximize their impact and benefit to our and others' well-being.

What Buddhism says about emotions is directly related to our actions and can provide guidance on how to live enriched lives. Understanding the mind, and our conduct in everyday life are intimately related. How we understand ourselves and how we behave cannot be separated. Relating to positive emotions well has the capacity to produce positive and virtuous actions in the individual. An increase in virtuous intention and action introduces a change in the character of the person.

From a Buddhist perspective, if we want to change ourselves, it should not be done in a superficial way, solely in terms of our mind, disassociated from our physical embodiment. It should include our character as well, because character is something that we possess not just in terms of our thoughts, emotions, beliefs, attitudes, and so on. It also involves how we carry ourselves, conduct ourselves, how we relate to other people, our activities, how we respond in times of difficulty, and so on. Our character displays our depth.

Relating to circumstances, even tragic ones, with as much

stability and positivity as possible adds depth to our being. This type of responsiveness builds strength and resilience, assisting us to face all kinds of difficulty, trauma, and disturbance more easily and with a clearer, less distorted state of mind. Such responsiveness should be accompanied by full-heartedness and sincerity.

It is often stated in Buddhist teachings that we should remain non-attached or dispassionate. These terms do not relate to non-emotionality. What is meant by "non-attachment" or "dispassion," as it is so often translated, references the ability to be non-attached and not motivated by anger, jealousy, spite, resentment, bitterness, and other negative manifestations. It suggests a type of composure that allows us to remain steady without being thrown by turbulent thoughts and emotions. So in this context, "being dispassionate" means we are not motivated by negative states of mind, and negative emotions. That then leads to a healthier way of behaving in everyday life. In that way, we are able to conduct ourselves in such a manner that we are able to lead an exemplary way of life—a life that is not always based on following cultural rules necessarily, or on following our attachments and attractions to negative habit-patterns.

Evaluating Benefit

There are many reasons why we try to do the right thing and behave appropriately. We often comply with religious rules and religious instruction, and this may be done without too much reflection or thought but be simply a case of following the rules. We may even try to do the right thing because we are concerned about the consequences of our behavior, due to a belief in karma and rebirth, or heaven and hell. Such thoughts and ideas can become motivating factors for good behavior. Goodness, virtue, and what is beneficial are all interrelated, according to this way of thinking.

Following predetermined rules of conduct without evaluating

what is beneficial in the immediate circumstances may result in our behaving in ways that are not helpful, and which may even cause harm. "Beneficial" here, refers to what brings happiness. So whatever brings real happiness and a real sense of joy to ourselves and others is something that we should try to pursue.

If we cultivate ourselves properly in relation to positive emotions and work with the negative emotions to reduce their impact in the way we have been describing, then we can become enriched, and our character can change and deepen. We become less superficial, not so easily persuaded this way and that, not unnecessarily affected by popularization, trends and fashion, whether referring to values, money, or acceptable behavior.

When we try to cultivate ourselves emotionally, develop good character, and learn to relate to everything and everyone more effectively, this approach is in contrast to following the religious and societal rules somewhat blindly without considering the nuances of the immediate situation and circumstances.

It is important to remember that whatever we experience, we do not experience in isolation. The way that we experience things and deal with them has an impact on others and that in turn, will have an impact on us. For example, generally speaking, when it comes to difficulties in life such as trauma, we might see a particular event as being the sole cause of our sensitivity or unhappiness. From a Buddhist point of view, a particular incident can be the catalyst, but our response to that incident is also affected by such influences as our propensities, underlying attitudes, strengths and weaknesses, relationship with others, and so on. So a traumatic incident is considered to be multifaceted and interconnected with who we are as a person, others in our lives, and the outer environment. Trauma is easily galvanized through subsequent triggers and reinforcements in various forms, including our relationship with others. This in turn, can reinforce a person's saṁskāras and continuum of being, which in Tibetan is called *rgyun*. That then impacts on our character. Such attitudes and responses could become deeply ingrained, and it could be difficult to overcome certain emotional problems, as they in time become who we believe we are and form a central part of our character[32].

Emotional experience is not just in the head; emotional experience is written on our face, manifests in behavior and attitude, feelings, how we see other people, how we carry ourselves and conduct our life, and how we behave. For these reasons alone it is important to address the repertoire, the whole assembly of our mental life, in terms of our attitudes, feelings, beliefs, and our character. Whatever our habit-patterns might be, not being too trusting, being paranoid, stingy and so on—our range of behaviors and habit-patterns impact on whether we are living fully or not and that is really what it all boils down to.

Fundamental change in our character is what we should strive for, not just some kind of relief from difficulties we have at the present time. Sometimes there is a need to seek external assistance to make our way through a difficult issue or intense time. That can be a legitimate approach to moving forward more positively with our life and I commend such efforts and activities, whether via Buddhist teachers and practices, psychologists, psychotherapists, counselors, or other forms of skilled assistance. From a Buddhist perspective, we still need to strive further. Being able to express our grief, loss, emotional issues, or whatever the difficulty might be, can help us to experience some relief, but our character may still remain unchanged. We should not be discouraged, particularly if we have managed to navigate even part of the way through a difficult situation. That is a great achievement and such relief should be acknowledged and celebrated. Having navigated through such intensity, we can still find that many of our unhelpful or diminishing behaviors and attitudes continue. Whatever our negative behavioral tendencies might be, such as being intolerant, selfish, resentful, jealous—these attitudes can very well continue to degrade our life. So the work of generating positivity through understanding the mind is essential for true transformation and character-building.

Buddhism does not see emotions as purely mental experiences. The individual and the ego, like phenomena, are seen as insubstantial and in a state of flux. The fullness of this idea is that from a personal perspective we have the ability to transform and our sense of self and ego can be fluid. We do not have to have a fixated sense of self, nor do we need to get rid of the ego. Generally speaking, the ego is helpful to be able to portray a consistent and considerate persona that is experienced by others as stable and reliable. In that sense, Buddhism does not recognize pure ego. Further, what constitutes ego is not unitary and should be understood as comprised of five psychophysical constituents:

—the physical aspect (*rūpa*),
—conceptual construct (*saṁjñā*),
—psychophysical predispositions (*saṁskāra*),
—feelings (*vedanā*),
—consciousness (*vijñāna*) or (*citta*)

So as with the mind and phenomena, we think of ego in terms of elements.

Like the emotions, Buddhism does not describe ego as something that is purely mental. Buddhism says ego should be understood in relation to the skandhas. It means that ego is not something that exists totally independent of the physical aspect or physical embodiment. So, physical aspects or rūpa includes many elements. To understand the sensory faculties we have to think in terms of a sensory object—a visual or nasal object, etcetera. It is linked to many different elements. So equally, ego is not a free-floating entity. Even what we think of as "the ego" is intertwined with our psychophysical constitution. If we understand ourselves in that way, then we are less likely to dissociate the mental from the physical. Further, we also avoid dissociating the physical from our behavior and interaction, in terms of our character, dispositions, propensities, and things of that kind.

To reiterate, Buddhism does not say we should just change the mind. What Buddhism says is we should change our character, and we should change our disposition. We should learn to become predisposed to respond to things in a different way. Then we can become a changed person. Self-transformation does not come from simply telling ourselves to see things differently, or have different feelings, or to try to have new emotions. Change comes fundamentally from teaching ourselves to become predisposed to accommodating things that we do not like, appreciating things that we take for granted, and moderating our excessive desire, excessive attraction, and excessive aversion. To clarify, we do not stop liking things; it is not about us not liking things. It is about knowing what we like, what we do not like, and to what extent we have attraction and aversion. We are looking at how our preferences can impact on the quality of our lives, and how extremes can debilitate our happiness and sense of fulfillment. Our propensities and how we respond to our experiences is all tied up with the positive emotions, positive mental factors, the negative mental factors, and negative emotions, listed earlier. While these ideas can at first glance seem complex, they are actually very grounded and straightforward. The practices need to be applied as we have been instructed so that we can work with our mental factors and emotions in a practical manner.

Buddhism says that we do not have to become virtuous or gain enlightenment overnight. As I have emphasized, even if we feel jealous or angry, we can dismantle the substructures that promote these strong negative forms of emotion. They will then diminish over a period of time. When we deal with the secondary negative emotions in that way, we reduce their strength and, in weakening them, gradually, as the suffering is reduced, our happiness will increase. In these practices there is no promise that we can stop being jealous or angry overnight. However, due to the interrelationship of the mind-elements, if for example, we learn to be less stingy and mean-spirited, that will automatically impact on our feelings of jealousy as well, and their impact will begin to be defused. That is the Buddhist view.

Although we may think different kinds of negative emotions are unrelated to each other, they are actually connected and related. If we relate to certain negative aspects of the substructure, if we can see some aspects strongly within ourselves, then the negative emotions that we want to overcome will have begun to respond or yield.

With positive emotions there are the natural positive emotions, positive emotions by association, by motivation, by subsequent relations, and ultimate positive emotional states. With negative emotions there are natural negative emotions, negative emotions by association, by motivation, and by subsequent relations. Here, we are reminded of the dharmas because the negative emotions or positive emotions do not exist in isolation. So, a natural virtue like love is not free-floating, because that virtue may arise in relation to other virtuous dispositional properties. Virtue may also arise because of a positive motivation such as wanting to help somebody, and then love arises as a consequence.

When we read how the positive and negative emotions and dispositions and so forth are described, it is important not to fall into the trap of becoming moralistic. Having positive motivation, intentions, and actions is not predetermined, from a Buddhist perspective. While guidelines are important, equally, for us to respond appropriately and in a way that increases happiness and reduces suffering for self and others, we need to understand the circumstance pertinent to the situation in which we wish to help. That is closer to what is meant in Buddhism as "being ethical." We need to consider the circumstances one is faced with. A fixed moral code of behavior may not provide the type of flexibility needed in multiple situations to achieve the best outcome for all.

One of my main intentions in sharing these teachings was to ensure that Buddhism is properly understood and recognized as a full path, not just a partial path which does not include the gamut of human experience, and to make sure it is appreciated that Buddhism is all about relationship. It is vital that, if we choose to, we can wholeheartedly practice Buddhism, in order to improve our lives. Understanding the Buddhist approach and addressing potential doubts may help to ensure that when we follow the Buddhist path our experience of life is not diminished because of a misinterpretation, but rather, enriched in every possible way. In Buddhism, desire is used as one of the greatest motivators on the path. By using positive desires and emotions we are enabled to relinquish or reduce the grip that negative states of mind can have over us. To recognize that working with the mind can be approached with equal effectiveness whether one is a lay practitioner or a monastic sangha member is also extremely valuable. Regardless of whether one is a renunciant or not, fundamentally what we are working on, in order to enrich our lives, is the same. Our task is to understand how the elements of the mind work together to create experience, and through knowing this, we can transform and enrich our lives and the lives of others.

Chapter 16
How Things Exist and How Things Appear

Buddhism supplies us with a map of the mind, which tells us how the mind works and how to navigate it. In conjunction with that, Buddhism has a lot to say about how our emotions arise, why they arise, and how we can understand and manage them, and then learn to lead a happier, more enriched and ethical life.

Fundamentally, the Buddhist approach to the mind and emotions in terms of our mental life has to do with the interconnection of many elements, as we have been discussing. The mind cannot be understood as a single entity and in isolation. Morality and ethics, the virtues that uplift us and the vices that degrade us, our emotional and psychological make-up, our physicality, and our character—everything is interconnected. If we are to speak about desire and our emotional make-up, then we have to understand this interconnection. Thus we need to understand the dharmas[33].

Speaking about the Dharmas

From a Buddhist perspective, when we work on our psychological and emotional states, our efforts should be directed towards building up certain strengths and qualities, and building and deepening our character. As samsaric beings, we develop into a certain type of individual as we become habituated to respond in consistent ways and as a result, we behave in a manner that creates a persona of one kind or another. In that way, our likes and dislikes, how we behave and respond to things, what we choose to do or not do, our hopes and fears, are all connected to our character. Our virtues and vices are related to our emotional and psychological states. They in turn, are related to our character, and determine how we behave.

Who we are and our response to circumstances are not completely predetermined of course. There is an element of determinism in terms of the way we are likely to respond because, according to the Buddhist way of thinking, the presumption is that we create much of our own suffering due to ignorance, and that our responses are highly habituated. Also relevant to the discussion is how our environment influences the way we develop. Living in a violent or alternatively, a harmonious neighborhood, being economically deprived or having economic abundance, and so on will all have an impact on who we are and become. There is, however, no fully predetermined outcome, and within each particular environment a multiplicity of individual outcomes arises based on our responses to differing circumstances.

At the basis of this whole discussion is the connection between emotional states, strength and depth of character, and between virtue and vice that leads to the kinds of actions we perform. Buddhism does not encourage viewing virtues and vices in purely moralistic terms. In the Buddhist context, "virtues and vices" does not refer to the need for us to follow rules, or do what is considered to be the "right thing." Rather, our virtues and vices should be understood as opportunities to choose actions that bring wholesome mental states and well-being to ourselves and others.

The reason we should behave in a way that is beneficial is not because we are simply performing our duty, but because we would enjoy our lives more. This is because we would then develop and enhance our character so that we would naturally or instinctively act in a way that is beneficial. We would also have more frequent experiences of emotions that are of a more comforting and nurturing nature, rather than disturbing and destabilizing.

For instance, if one is mean-spirited, covetous, unforgiving, and resentful, then one ends up with a character that is unable to enjoy life, or to give and receive love. One can actually be unable to build a sound relationship with others, both in terms of indulging in an unsound way of thinking, and having strong tendencies to be entangled in negative emotions. Such an individual would be in a state of turmoil, not knowing how to establish relationships with others, or even with themselves. Therefore, whatever that person does, would be either offensive or upsetting to others or have a negative impact. So, from the Buddhist point of view, our emotional well-being is connected to our psychological make-up, depth of character, and how we behave.

In such situations, we might convince ourselves that there are scenarios that would "fix" everything.

We might think, "If I could do that, then I could be very successful. I'd have all the money I wanted and if I had money, I could do whatever I wanted. I could live wherever I wanted, I could attract people and they would want to know me. I'd be able to have good relationships with others because they would want to be with me, due to all that I could give them." These types of beliefs are not worthwhile if we follow them and end up with a weak character— lacking ethical fortitude and insight. Then, far from the result we expected, we would not experience emotional health or be happy within ourselves. We can always find somebody or something to blame for our misery. A person of weak character is someone who will always find an excuse and somebody to blame. That is not the way to go, according to the Buddhist view. Having said that, to be taking personal responsibility and at the same time, holding people to account when required, is not a contradiction. Such positioning can also be a demonstration of character-building.

When we speak about virtues and vices in the Buddhist context, it has nothing to do with sin. Vice does not have to be affiliated with sin, in this connection. It does not have to be linked to a notion of having disobeyed a supreme being who is watching and judging us, nor is it connected to a set of rules we must comply with. It is, nevertheless, related to what Buddhism teaches about emotions because there are many different ways to behave and be. When we talk about psychological and emotional states, we are talking about a state of being. When we talk about virtues, vices, and an ethical way of being, we are referring to action. There has to be coordination between being and doing yet, often, there is no coordination. The tension between the two leads people to experience all manner of trauma, suffering, and pain. There may be little compatibility between who they are, what they want to do, and how they are doing something or acting. According to Buddhism, this incompatibility leads to unhappiness. One of the fundamental aspects of what is being discussed in this book has to do with whether or not there is coordination and compatibility. Part of our goal in creating inner peace is to try to attain this at whatever level of coordination and compatibility we can.

Beyond that, in Mahayana, there is the notion that we need to make a distinction between *how things are in reality*—which refers to ultimate reality or things being empty of inherent existence, in short "emptiness"; and how things exist on a day-to-day level, what can refer to as relative truth or our "empirical experience." These two are known in Buddhism as the "two truths."

This notion of two truths—ultimate and relative truth—has roots in what we have already covered in terms of "dharmas" or dependently arising mental and physical phenomena. I have emphasized that we normally think of emotions as being unitary and that from a Buddhist perspective, our emotional life is not unitary but made up of various elements. We may think, "I'm getting emotional," but the teachings say that if we look into *who* is emotional, then there is not a single thing called "I" who gets emotional. That "I" is composed of our physical aspect: there is a body of a certain shape, weight, height, age, and a particular racial background, cognitive capacities and feelings—and they all come together. What is the ultimate truth and relative truth on that level? If we understand the interconnection of all things in this manner, we will have an understanding of ultimate truth, and of the insubstantial and changeable nature of all things.

As far as the relative truth is concerned, when we interact in the world, we often have little experiences of the interconnection of things, and less knowledge of where experience resides. We actually may not see our own emotional state as being central to our experience. We think of outer events and external circumstances as the most significant as if my own emotional response is something added on to what has happened to me. All of these things have to do with how the dharmas are playing out, so to speak—how all these dharmas are being organized in our mind. This involves matters like where to place the blame or how to interpret the world and all of our experiences.

According to Mahayana, we have to understand phenomena and our experience of them in terms of how things exist and how things appear. "How things exist" is not "how things appear." "How things are" is not actually so very interesting, in a way. "How things appear" is interesting, full of promise but also of peril, because it appears so solid, unitary, and it is imbued with our habitual way of seeing things. In Mahayana, how things are is emptiness—which means lacking inherent existence, being insubstantial, and having the nature of *śūnyatā*[34].

"Promise" in this context, is in terms of what we really want in life on the empirical level. So, on the empirical level, we want certain things, and do not want other things. We want a relationship with certain people but not with others, and so on. Through our senses, we grasp and attach onto certain things we perceive as valuable and we become fixated. In Mahayana Buddhism, we refer to this aspect as "the appearance of things" or "appearance." If we look at this notion, "the appearance of things," we will see that it is connected to the idea of dharmas. The "appearance of things" is the dharmas. So that means that what we experience on the physical, mental, and emotional levels are all appearances. They are called "appearances" because we have imbued an object with a range of attributes that relates to our sets of attractions and aversions. Whether the item or the individual contains those qualities we have attributed to them, is the question. Normally, we have superimposed our dharmas onto the object that then distorts our experience. Therefore, we do not see these particular things from an undistorted perspective and that gives rise to conflicting emotions. If we could see appearances as they are, free of distortion, not existing in the way we experience them, thus recognizing their insubstantial quality, then this would not give rise to emotional affliction.

What we need to understand as well, is that simply because the distortion of appearances is self-generated, it does not mean that we should then suppress our responsive engagement with life. We do not need to disregard how we feel about our relationships with things, people, social environments, and so on, because in reality they have no real substance or basis. This of course is not the case but rather it is the converse. It is so important that we develop an understanding of the relationship between how things are and how they appear. How things are and how things appear cannot be separated. The way that they appear is because of how things are. So, from the point of view of Mahayana Buddhism, as human beings, even in terms of our emotional life, it is not the case that we should only think in terms of how things exist in reality, and not concern ourselves with how things appear empirically or rationally. How things appear and how things exist, are intimately related, but generally we do not experience the world in this way. We tend to think that how things appear is how things exist. As long as we think in that way, conflicting emotions will arise because of our assumption that what we perceive or how we experience things is real and solid.

When we are doing meditation, we tend to think that whatever we are experiencing should be used as a yardstick to judge what is going on, but Mahayana and early Buddhism do not say that. What is said is that we have to rely on our experience but our experience has to be measured against our understanding of how things actually exist. Since we are deluded beings, we do not know how things actually exist from an experiential level. We may read about emptiness, interdependent origination, and so on, but we do not know or experience the world and ourselves in that way normally.

The fundamental point is that in Mahayana Buddhism, we talk about two levels of reality and two levels of perception. To understand how things are, we need the support of a number of mental faculties. One of these faculties of mind is faith or conviction. We do not know "how things are." Whatever instruction and advice has come from the Buddha, and enlightened practitioners such as Nagarjuna and Shantideva on the Indian side, and Longchenpa and Karmapa Rangjung Dorje on the Tibetan side, is informed guidance that we need to look closely at. To a large degree, we need to take seriously what they have to say regarding enlightenment and the path. If we are unable to take this kind of instruction and advice with careful attention and follow it with vigor, it will impede our progress and capacity to understand what Buddhism speaks about in relation to ultimate reality. This does not suggest that we should be gullible, or vacuously follow instructions. It is important to emphasize that real transformation occurs through strong motivation and genuine engagement.

As a Buddhist, if we take notice of what the Buddha and traditional enlightened practitioners say, it will greatly enhance our ability to relate to and understand the world. Our personal impressions and our experiences have failed to give us the full picture, so we need to heed what the enlightened beings have said. We need advice both from the buddhas and our own experiences.

Buddhism emphasizes that we should not rely on the Buddha to validate our experiences. How we experience must become validated through investigating our own experiences. To explain, once we have started to put trust in what the Buddha has said, the theory needs to be tested in relation to our own experience—in meditation and post-meditation—to avoid such things as blind-faith and dogmatism arising, and to build a proper understanding and insight into the human condition. We cannot test how we experience, discovering the many interconnected elements by proxy through theoretical understanding to see if it conforms to our personal experiences. This type of testing needs to be accompanied by a thorough understanding of the Dharmic approach[35].

It is important to have an intelligent approach to Buddhism however that does not mean that faith is inessential. Building faith and conviction, through listening to and reading the texts of the masters is part of an intelligent approach, and it can be an effective antidote to emotional affliction. Early and Mahayana Buddhism put a great deal of emphasis on faith. That is because there is a lot that we do not know when we begin and start to progress on the path, so we listen to the greater authorities. In Mahayana, how we use reason and logic to understand reality and relate to the world determines our emotional state. For example, if we are feeling emotional, we can think about the processes culminating in our becoming emotional. We can apply three kinds of resources in order to get a better handle on what we are going through so that our emotional state can become more stable and less disturbed or exaggerated. Firstly, we can consider the interconnected nature of everything, secondly, that what we experience is not the whole picture, and thirdly, we remind ourselves that in reality everything is lacking a permanent intrinsic nature, is insubstantial and thus transformative. That is, one is trying to have an understanding of what the Buddha has said to help relate to what is going on when we are feeling a sense of confusion or bewilderment. These contemplations and considerations give us the background information we need to clarify what is happening in the mind.

Using this background information helps us identify how and where we have lost perspective.

For example, we recognize we are angry with someone, that they made us feel very hurt, and we feel let down. So initially, we see the complexity of what has happened and the many responses we have had in relation to it. The deeper we go, the more complexity we can experience. When we do not examine the interconnected components that culminate in our experience, but rather focus on the end product, the experience itself, it is difficult to gain any insight. It can become black and white, this person made me angry. Then there is no notion of interdependent arising, or insubstantiality arising within our thought patterns. We think, "I know what's going on—this has happened." However, when we apply the three resources and look into our experience holistically, we see that it is not simple. We come to the understanding that everything comes from dharmas and they are without essence.

We can see the experiences arise in relation to varieties of factors, hence the complexity. If our anger, jealousy, and so forth had an essence, there would be no complexity. It would then be very simple. The very fact that they are not "simple" on the level of appearance, and the varieties of ways we experience that appearance—shows that there is no essence.

What we regard as anger or jealousy or the like changes from one circumstance to another. We may experience jealousy in relation to a colleague who has just been promoted instead of us. We may also feel jealousy in relation to another situation that is completely unconnected to that, and then the whole flavor, tone, or intensity of the jealousy is different. So from a Mahayana point of view, all jealousies are not the same. There are different forms, many different jealousies and likewise, many different angers. There are many versions of every emotion. To make things simpler, our mind groups these emotional responses together to create some order and make sense of things. The information coming in through our senses and our responses to them are normally organized into a range of categories. So there are many types of angers that fall under the one category of anger, or jealousies under the category of jealousy.

When we are going through life, we do not always have the time to process all the information that is coming through our senses. So we have to make quick judgments about things and sometimes they serve us well, but often, they do not. We become habituated in such a way that our thinking and deciding process becomes more automated and less visible, to the point of being invisible. Mahayana Buddhism says if we recognize this, we will have some spaciousness to judge less quickly habitually. We can develop the opportunity to respond differently and experience things freshly. Vipaśyanā or analytical meditation is designed to assist in the process of piecing apart the processes that lead to a response.

From a Mahayana perspective, in vipaśyanā or analytical meditation, we are trying to learn how to operate from the relative and absolute point of view in order to integrate the two perspectives of seeing how things are, and how things appear. Developing the coordination within the two perspectives of relative and absolute truth is done in conjunction with learning about the dharmas, the interconnection of the many mental and physical factors.

One needs to develop the understanding that there is no separation between the appearance and how we experience the appearance, and its insubstantial essence. If there were essence or substantiality, then appearance would be consistent. For example, there would be one essential unchanging state called anger and then we would be able to say with certainty, "this is anger," or we could say "this is jealousy, and this is hatred." But, as we know, it does not happen that way. It is like looking at whole species of vegetables such as peppers or tomatoes—they are all different. We say "vegetables," but they are not all the same. The same thing happens in the garden of our mind. This is seen as extremely important from a Buddhist point of view.

In our discussion we have examined renunciation and detachment and also the importance of relationship, and noted that it is a misunderstanding to say that Buddhism focuses on the individual and does not emphasize relationship. In early Buddhism there would not have been an emphasis on learning about the dharmas, appearance or relative truth *samvritisatya* in sanskrit, and *kun rdzob bden pa* in Tibetan, if relationship were not important. Buddhism presents the idea that if we renounce certain ways of relating to the world, we can establish a better and more realistic relationship with the world and others. Buddhism has always considered relationships, emotional well-being, and other positive human capacities as important and very valuable.

If we see the relationship between how things are and how things appear in proper perspective, based on our understanding of the dharmas and our understanding of interrelationship, then there will be emotional color. The color will be vivid, penetrating, enriching and very moving. Different levels of realization are described in very colorful terms, quite literally. It is not like we are being asked to understand something like two and two equals four. On the contrary, if we understand the non-separation of appearance and reality, we are developing a new way of seeing the world, which is full of possibility and meaning. Our vision, as it were, will open up.

Whether we are talking about early Buddhism, or about Mahayana Buddhism, we are advised not to pay too much attention to our sensory inputs, or allow ourselves to get overly worked up about what we perceive. That does not mean we should ignore the sensory input but rather, that our responses should be managed and moderated. Whether responding to what comes to us through the senses or in relation to such emotions as desire, we need to manage the intensity of our grasping and fixation to enhance our experience of life. Our unbridled intensity can not only lead to fixation, but even to our becoming insatiable and getting into trouble, as was thoroughly discussed in Part 1. So when we speak of renunciation here, it refers to us renouncing some of the ways we have been relating to the world. Such a position will not only assist in the management and understanding of our responses and desires, but it is a significant way of progressing on the spiritual path.

Renunciation is not an approach to looking at everything in the world as being insignificant, totally distracting, vile, or something to get rid of or to escape from. That is not the Buddhist view. The Buddhist view is that what we should escape from is the world of make-believe that is based on our exaggerated expectations and frustrations. That means that we should renounce our expectation that the world can deliver more than it can, since this is how the samsaric state is perpetuated.

Learning to deal with the world in a way that is more in correspondence with what the world can actually deliver is the bodhisattva way of life. That is the Mahayana vision, which is based on us relating to a world that corresponds with how things truly are, and not getting too worked up in our response to the world, a response based on our fantasies, frustrations, and expectations. This does not mean the Mahayana world is devoid of color. The concept of emptiness does not mean nothingness. This is a very important distinction.

In Buddhism with descriptions of "meditative experiences" and "realizations"—that is, emotional responses and cognitive understanding, respectively—go together and that is how we develop an understanding of how appearance and reality co-exist. If we understand things that way, then our emotional repertoire will be more far-ranging. We have become habituated, and we will continue to respond to things in the same or similar ways, emotionally and cognitively, as we get older. In effect, our range of experiences and ways of responding will become more and more limited and, over time, instead of becoming more resourceful, we would actually become more habituated and narrowly focused, and therefore, we would suffer more.

So the Mahayana view is that if we understand how things exist and how things appear, and understand the interconnection between the two, this will open things up more.

We will be able to express ourselves emotionally in a more creative fashion, with some kind of sensibility, which is not to be equated with being rational. Responding to things in a purely rational manner may not be so sensible. Similarly, responding to things in a completely emotional way may not necessarily be sensible either. So, we are exercising sense and sensibility, but not the way Jane Austen did with *Sense and Sensibility*!

When there is harmony between reason, rationality, and emotions, then we have sense. Doing that involves balancing the perspective of how things appear on the empirical level, and how things exist—to use Kant's notion of *noumenon*—these two realms of the empirical or nominal or the perspective of reality of how things exist. That harmonization of these two basically involves using wisdom on a lower level and wisdom on a higher level. Wisdom on a lower level is called *prajñā* and using it on a higher level is called *jñāna*[36]. The aim of Mahayana Buddhism is that our prajñā will become more and more proximate to jñāna. Until we attain jñāna, the wisdom mind, all we can do is use our prajñā, our sensibility, as much as we can so that we do not become totally unemotional in the process of trying to overcome negative emotions. It is important to ensure we do not get cut off from our emotions, or desensitize ourselves. Equally important is to not become completely emotional and lose our capacity to think clearly and reason through things. We need both capacities—both are essential.

Mahayana Buddhism also uses many other methods, such as the practice of loving-kindness meditation[37], designed to counteract negative tendencies. We can only make sense of our experiences fully if we are familiar with distinctions between positive and negative desire and the gamut of emotional responses, and the multiplicity of elements that come together to create human experience, because the Mahayana notion of cultivating loving-kindness is based on the understanding that our mind has many aspects. As human beings, we are not just one thing. Therefore, trying to work with different aspects of our mind, propensities, tendencies, and habits is what is required, but not all at once. Otherwise the process of increasing our self-knowledge and efforts to transform and elevate ourselves can be come unruly, overwhelming, and tend towards excessive self-criticism. The process should be, while challenging, also uplifting.

So we can be aware of something we wish to change, while we are working on another aspect of ourselves. For example, our main focus could be working on building up a more positive attitude towards being generous, so we develop positivity around the idea of being generous in such activities as observing our mind more carefully in meditation, helping friends more, spending time with family, giving to our local charities and so on—while in the background, we are aware of our tendency to be impatient. That would be enough focus on the tendency to be impatient, while working more directly on reducing our tendency to be miserly, by being more generous. Giving some attention and thought to the idea of change can plant a seed. It can plant the seed in our mind that will cause us to improve our behavior simply though acknowledging such a shortcoming. We should not underestimate the importance of a thought. The idea is that positive emotions will follow if the right thought is there. So if we learn to think kindly of someone or ourselves, kindness will follow. If we are thinking badly of someone or ourselves, then the negative emotions will become intensified.

So we work on whichever characteristics or propensities in our character we feel need more immediate attention. In that way we can experience real progress. The desire to improve is a very positive motivation and is enough to begin the process of change. The Mahayana view is that it makes sense to think about the power of thought, in conjunction with what we would like to change within ourselves, but often we do not see the beginnings of change as happening so easily. If we recognize the power of thought to instigate change, then change is closer and the process of change less daunting than we may think. Change for the better requires positive and fresh ways of thinking. It does not take very long for us to think badly of somebody we, at one time, thought kindly of—a person disappoints us and a negative thought enters our mind, takes root, grows, and then hatred can follow. The use of a positive thought provides the right environment for positive emotions to arise naturally.

Mahayana Buddhism has a very intelligent approach to transforming the human condition. Meditational and contemplative exercises take our mental tendencies and habitual tendencies into account. We work with our tendencies to create a more positive environment for beautiful positive qualities such as loving-kindness to flourish. For example, it may be difficult to think kindly of some people that we know, so in a meditation exercise, we are asked to generate loving-kindness towards other people we do not know so well, first, or even those we have never met. Then once we have generated loving-kindness quite intensely to humanity broadly, we can then turn to directing that towards people we have a history with to generate a more non-judgmental and comprehensive love. The interesting thing is that we often do not love our loved ones in the appropriate manner that leads to our or their emotional health. The idea is to extend our capacity to connect and be more fully in relationship. In Mahayana we seek to learn to love both enemies and friends. Not naively but in terms of the recognition of the importance of truly being in relationship with ourselves, others, and the world[38].

Thinking along these lines allows us to see how the Buddhist approach can transform us on an emotional level in a very practical way. This is because there is such a wealth of information within the Dharma and there are many practices that we can do to specifically defuse and repair very emotional states. On a very practical level, of course, there are many ways to manage pressing emotional issues. By talking to one's teacher or spiritual guide, with friends, or using other therapies if one wishes, all can defuse some of the tension, and prevent potential compounding issues. Addressing a pressing issue is important and when addressed effectively, should relieve some of the immediate pressure. However, to really transform, a depth of thinking and consideration about the complexity of the human condition is required. Recognizing the power of thought to initiate inner change, contemplating the nature of appearance and reality, and the interconnectedness of all things can truly transform. That was Buddha's very rich message handed down through the generations. Every aspect of Buddhism is interconnected precisely because of this notion of dharmas. If you understand that everything is dependent on dharmas, then you will understand that the methods to work with the dharmas are also diverse but interconnected.

Therefore, just leading a good or moral life is not the ultimate and neither is leading a contemplative life or a life of meditation. All of these things have to be brought to bear, even in terms of believing in the Buddha and his teachings. We often cannot reason our way through difficulties because of our limited understanding of our own situation and the human condition more broadly. Studying the Buddha's words and the associated texts, we can expand our understanding. Understanding the teachings is important, but without thinking about and contemplating these things thoroughly, it would still be a shortcoming. Reasoning, without proper understanding can also lead us astray. If one has decided to really look into Buddhism, it is best to develop a thorough understanding through studying the teachings and through meditational practices.

In Buddhism there are many views and they are interconnected. The different aspects of the discussion presented here are not purely intellectual and abstract but directly relate to our emotional well-being. In Buddhism we are not wanting to be simply a rational person, but rather a sensible one. A sensible person is what one should try to learn to become. No aspect of the human condition can be left out on our spiritual journey. We use everything on the path to enlightenment. It is important to be fully engaged and to embrace what it is to be human. The power of desire can uplift us and lead us to experience a fuller and greater sense of ourselves and to embrace humanity and our own humanness. Managing the complexity of being human and through such management achieving self-improvement and transformation is its own art form. Strength, resilience, and courage are all essential on the path. It can be said that perfection lies in our ability to have a connection with that which is not perfect.

Notes

PART 1

1. Dharmic Path, means to follow the Dharma. Dharma refers to Buddhist teachings. The "three turnings of the wheel of Dharma" for example, refers to the 3 main teachings of the Buddha on the concept of emptiness or reality—how things exist. The first turning was the Buddha's teachings on impermanence or emptiness. The second turning was referring to the teachings on the impermanent and empty nature of phenomena. That is, the idea of the impermanent nature of both the self and phenomena. The third turning related to Tathagatagarbha, or Buddha Nature. Here Buddha Nature was explained as being an untainted and incorruptible state. Kyabgon, Traleg, *The Essence Of Buddhism*, Shambhala Publications, 2001, p. 131.

2. Grasping and fixation are discussed in detail particularly in part 1 of this book. In brief, grasping or clinging is seen as coming from not knowing how to handle our emotional responses and experiences. Fixation in this context is defined as the intellectual component that holds onto certain ideas, beliefs, likes and dislikes, etcetera in a somewhat obsessive way, within a conceptual framework. Fixation attempts to solidify our responses to certain experiences. Therefore our thought processes and responses can become highly habitualized. The intensity of our grasping and fixation relates to the management of desire: enhancing positive desires, and reducing the effect of excessive and negative desires and their destructive outcomes.

3. See note 2 for a brief explanation of grasping and fixation.

4. In brief the twelve dependent links, also known as the twelve interdependent links are a chain of events that include: habitual grasping and fixation on mental events and phenomena, apprehension of objects via the sense consciousnesses; desire, feelings of attraction, aversion and neutrality towards experiences etcetera. The idea is to break the samsaric cycle by developing an intimate understanding of the twelve links. It is believed understanding how the samsaric mind works, developing our knowledge of the activity of the samsaric mind, and through developing mindfulness and awareness, we can break the chain of events that perpetuate samsara. Grasping, fixations, and desire are discussed in part 1 of this book. Buddhist psychology in relation to building awareness of how the mind works including sense consciousnesses and how we apprehend phenomena is discussed in more detail in part 2 of this book.

5. Mahayana Buddhism is often described as a later form of Buddhism. The Mahayana perspective is not determined by doctrine, school, or belief but by the internal attitude of the practitioner. The Mahayanist's attitude does not only seek enlightenment for oneself but for all sentient beings. Kyabgon,Traleg. *The Essence of Buddhism*, Shambhala Publications, 2001, P. 36-37.

6. Shantideva was a famous Indian scholar and yogi in the 8th century. He attended Nalanda University and wrote the profound and well-known text *Bodhicharyavatara*, whose title is translated as "A Guide to the Bodhisattva's Way of Life."

7. Kyabgon, Traleg. Karma, *What it is, What it isn't, Why it matters*, Shambhala Publications, 2015, provides a comprehensive explanation of karma from a number of perspectives.

8. There are many teachings and aspects to mindfulness from a Buddhist perspective. Essentially, mindfulness is a technique that is applied to meditation to build concentration, insight, and awareness. Mindfulness can be described as a process of observation. In śamatha or tranquility meditation, mindfulness is essentially a discipline that returns the mind back to the object of meditation when it wanders, thus building a more disciplined and concentrated or less distracted mind. In Vipashyana or analytical meditation mindfulness is applied in a different way to shamatha or tranquility meditation. With vipaśyanā, it is used as an aid to understanding how the mind works. An example of a mindfulness practice in vipaśyanā is the "four foundations of insight" where one applies mindfulness in four different ways in meditation: mindfulness of body, mindfulness of feelings, mindfulness of the mind, and mindfulness of conditioned existence.

9. The Four Noble Truths are:
    The Truth of Suffering or its converse The Truth of Happiness
    The Origin of Suffering or its converse The Origin of Happiness
    The Goal, the Cessation of Suffering or its converse The Perpetuation of Happiness (Nirvana)
    The Path, the Way Out of Suffering or its converse The Path To Happiness

10. Dependent Arising—refers to the idea that nothing in the world or our mind arises independently without causes and conditions. For a thought or an experience to arise, or for something in the world to manifest is due to a range of interconnected causes and conditions.

11. It is important to note the different meanings of "Dharma" and lower case "d," dharmas. Dharma (see note 1) refers to the

teachings of the Buddha. It also refers to Dharma practice, or practicing Dharma through meditation and actions. Lower case "d" "dharmas" means "all dependently or interdependently arising phenomena." In the context of this book, the author is discussing mental and physical elements predominantly. As stated, these are called "dharmas" in Buddhism. Another way to put it is that the idea of interconnecting of events and fields are called "dharmas."

12. Subjective idealism is a philosophical term based on the premise that nothing exists except mind and the mind's perceptions or ideas. A person experiences material things, but their existence is not independent of the perceiving mind; material things are thus mere perceptions. The fundamental idea related to this philosophy is that the outside world is contingent on a knower.

13. Logical positivism, also called logical empiricism, was a philosophical movement that arose in Vienna in the 1920s and was characterized by the view that scientific knowledge is the only kind of factual knowledge and that all traditional metaphysical doctrines are to be rejected as meaningless. Logical positivism believed that the ultimate basis of knowledge rests upon public experimental verification or confirmation rather than upon personal experience.

14. *Satipaṭṭhāna* meditation - The Satipaṭṭhāna Sutta provides the discourse on how to establish the foundations of mindfulness in meditation.

15. The relative level has to do with the day-to-day level of existence and experience. The ultimate level, also referred to, is the level of enlightened or ultimate view, such as seeing things as they truly exist in an untainted, undistorted, and uncontrived way.

16. Equilibrium does not indicate non-responsiveness. Equilibrium refers to not being thrown off-balance by anexperience. The experience is embraced more openly when freeor freer of grasping and fixation.

17. Thing-hood or thing-ness, from a Buddhist perspective, refers to the mistaken idea that things have a solid essence. Beyond the features, functionality, or characteristics of the object that help us to group similar things together creating conceptual categories, is a samsaric belief that things are unitary and independent. That is, things are not seen from an interdependent perspective, as containing many elements, causes, and condition. The perceiver may recognizes the common, as well as distinctive functions and characteristics of a thing in order to assist with the categorization process, e.g. such as a tables or chairs; anger or sadness, and so on, but the thing itself is seen as independently arising, from the samsaric perspective.

18. Five psychophysical constituents are also known as the five aggregates, or the five skandhas. They are: matter or body, which are the elements earth, space, fire, and water in a manifest form; feeling or sensations, more physically based; perception of a sense object; mental activity; and consciousness.

19. Nagarjuna—(1st-2nd century A.D.) One of the principle founders of Mahayana Buddhism and the Indian philosopher who founded the Madhyamaka School after he systemized and deepened the teachings of the *Perfection of Wisdom* sutras. Arguably the most influential Indian Buddhist thinker after Gautama Buddha, he provided the most comprehensive and methodological presentation of the Buddhist notion of emptiness.

20. Both Mahamudra and Dzogchen are often translated as the Great Seal or Great Perfection. Mahamudra is predominantly practiced in the Kagyu school of Tibetan Buddhism and is recognized as the highest yoga tantra. Unlike many other tantric practices, the practice of Mahamudra can be done free of ritual, but with detailed instruction on how to refine the mind in meditation. Ritualized tantric practices can be imbued with the quality or view of Mahamudra. The Mahamudra tradition advocates a direct meditative experience into the nature of the mind as a means of attaining the experience of "luminous bliss." In Mahamudra, the nature of the mind is not seen as the potential for enlightenment but rather as enlightenment itself. That is, the ability to remain in our natural or primordial state, untainted. Dzogchen, mainly practiced in the Nyingma school of Tibetan Buddhism, is also considered as the highest yoga tantra and has many parallels and similarities to Mahamudra. In Dzogchen one's goal is equally, to remain in one's natural state—the primordial state, or Buddha Nature.

21. In the Mahayana tradition Buddha-intentionality is referring to the practitioner's or Bodhisattva's desire to live for the benefit of other beings. The desire to reach enlightenment is done with that same intention. Generally speaking, everyday intentions can be defiled or undefiled, self-centered or other-centered or a combination defiled and undefiled etcetera. So the Mahayanist works towards becoming undefiled and other-centered. In order to do that, a Mahayana practitioner needs to become fully conscious or fully evolved.

PART 2

22. The whole of Buddha's teachings are collected into three major collections—Sutra, Vinaya, and Abhidharma. Sutric teachings

deal with Buddha's discourses, Vinaya sets out the monastic rules and regulations, and Abhidharma deals with Buddhist psychology and metaphysics.

23. See Note 11 for an explanation of the difference between Dharma and dharmas.

24. The author notes that mental events or mental factors are not good translations, but it is difficult to find words with equivalent meaning in English. The author has decided to use these terms, as they are commonly used by other translators.

25. This gradual approach to overcoming negative emotions in part 2 can be loosely paralleled with the graduated steps to overcoming fixation on views in part 1; wrong view can be paralleled with negative emotions supported by negative mental events; gradually adopting the right view can be paralleled with positive emotions classified as either defiled or undefiled; and non-view can be paralleled with completely undefiled emotions.

26. Saṁskāra is a sanskrit term meaning mental events, mental states or dispositional characteristics that influence our experience when apprehending an object. Habitual tendencies eventually become deeply ingrained to form our general disposition.

27. Often "kleśa" is translated as "emotions" but the author here suggests that "kleśa" refers only to negative forms of emotion.

28. Lojong literally means *training the mind*. An important part of Lojong practice is a series of slogans used for contemplation designed to redirect how we normally think, moving away from an egocentric perspective and towards generating bodhicitta or enlightened heart for all sentient beings. The Lojong teachings were developed from the principal Kadampa

master Atisha Dipamkara Shrijnana (982- 1054). Kyabgon, Traleg. *The Practice of Lojong*, Shambhala Publications, USA, 2007.

29. More information about such practices can be found in, Kyabgon, Traleg. Mind at Ease, Shambhala Publications, USA, 2004.

30. The term Dharmic values, here, refers to developing clear mindedness through understanding how the mind works. That is, one develops faith and conviction in some of the central tenants of Buddhism, such as dependent arising and insubstantiality or emptiness in order to understand the mind. This also is done to help maintain an other-centered focus, and a state of mind intent on acting in a way that builds enrichment and avoids harming others and oneself.

31. Nine stages of śamatha or tranquility meditation have been referred to in brief as: resting the mind; continuous resting; gather thoughts, emotions and concepts; pacification; subjugation; thorough subjugation; one-pointedness; and, sedative absorption. A full explanation of the nine stages of śamatha meditation can be found in book: Kyabgon, Traleg. *Moonbeams of Mahamudra*, Shogam Publications, Australia, 2015.

32. See note 26 for a brief description of saṁskāra.

33. "Dharmas" means "all dependently arising phenomena." Mental and physical phenomena are called "dharmas" in Buddhism. By having that knowledge, and not getting fixated on any one dharma is important developmentally on the Buddhist path. Realizing the many dharmas—seeing things as having many events, elements and factors, rather than seeing things from a myopic or unitary perspective. The many

interconnecting events, elements and factors are called "dharmas"—that understanding, in itself is considered transformative.

34. Śūnyatā is often translated as emptiness meaning the pervasive reality, free of inherent existence.

35. That approach as described, when investigating our experience, is different from and in contrast to trying to make our own experiences conform to certain commands or commandments. This can be the approach within some theistic religions. The author makes this point of contrast between Buddhism and some religions to help define the Buddhist approach, not to enter into a comparative religious dialogue *per se*. Such comments were made with great respect to the various religious traditions.

36. Wisdom is referred to as: *prajñā*. Prajñā is cultivated through meditation and links to the ability to generate ethical conduct through understanding which states of mind are beneficial and which are harmful; wisdom, a part of the ultimate state of being called *jñāna*—is the eventual state of the all encompassing wisdom mind.

37. Loving-kindness meditation, is also known as the Four Brahmavihāras. Meditators contemplate and generate the four virtues of love, sympathetic joy, equanimity and compassion, first towards oneself and then towards others. Kyabgon, Traleg. The *Essence Of Buddhism*, Shambhala Publications, USA, 2001.

38. In Buddhism, contrary to what some may believe, following a spiritual path such as is being presented here is not about *not* having anything to do with people because the world is samsaric and illusory and we have to run away from illusion

and attain buddhahood, seeing it as a trans-worldly state disconnected from anything to do with experience. That is not the Buddhist view. The Buddhist view is to create better relationships with oneself, others, and the world. We work towards being an undivided person, and to see and experience the interconnection with others and the world.

Index